GLOUCESTER'S
PAST IN PICTURES

by Caroline Baytop Sinclair

THE DONNING COMPANY
PUBLISHERS

Copyright © 1991 by Caroline Baytop Sinclair
All rights reserved, including the right to reproduce this work in any form whatsoever without permission in writing from the publisher, except for brief passages in connection with a review. For information, write:

The Donning Company/Publishers
184 Business Park Drive, Suite 106
Virginia Beach, VA 23462

B. L. Walton, Jr., Project Director
Richard A. Horwege, Editor
Mary Eliza Midgett, Designer
Holly B. Nuechterlein, Project Research Coordinator
Elizabeth B. Bobbitt, Pictorial Coordinator

Library of Congress Cataloging in Publication Data:
Sinclair, Caroline Baytop
  Gloucester's past in pictures / by Caroline Sinclair.
    p. cm.
  Includes bibliographical references (p.) and index.
  ISBN 0-89865-830-6
    1. Gloucester County (Va.)—History. 2. Gloucester County (Va.)—Description and travel—Views. I. Title.
F232.G6S55 1991   91-33153
975.5'32—dc20   CIP
Printed in the United States of America

Peninsula Trust Bank is pleased to make available this limited edition of Gloucester's Past in Pictures. We recognize that this land along the Chesapeake Bay and its tributaries has been bequeathed to us by many generations of loyal and industrious people. These characteristics can be found in the citizens of Gloucester today. These are the people who have placed their confidence in Peninsula Trust Bank and have helped us to grow solidly in this great community.

Special thanks to Caroline Baytop Sinclair for her timeless efforts in making this book the beautiful tribute that it is. Her careful documentation has preserved our history into something that will benefit each of us, as well as future generations.

We are proud to share this legacy and the belief that it will be treasured by those to whom it is entrusted.

William J. Farinholt, President & CEO

Dredging for oysters came late to Virginia and is still thought by some to be detrimental to the oyster beds, but it is now a regular practice within the oyster industry. Courtesy of the Virginia Institute of Marine Science.

Table of Contents

Preface 6
Acknowledgments 7
Introduction 9

CHAPTER ONE
The Colonial Period: 1607–1776 11

CHAPTER TWO
Revolution and Independence: 1776–1808 33

CHAPTER THREE
"Before the War:" 1808–1861 43

CHAPTER FOUR
Struggle and Rehabilitation: 1861–1890 57

CHAPTER FIVE
Recovery: 1890–1917 73

CHAPTER SIX
Two World Wars: 1917–1945 95

CHAPTER SEVEN
Changing Times: 1945–1990 127

CHAPTER EIGHT
Gloucester's Special Characteristics 165

Bibliography 202
Index 203
About the Author 208

Interior of Vaughan's Store at the Court House. The stove, the chair and the available newspapers indicate that shopping here is a leisurely occupation. The young man in suit and tie is certainly waiting for customers and the young black boy is obviously in no hurry. The calendar reads January 3, 1911. Courtesy of Gloucester Historical Committee

Preface

This pictorial presentation of Gloucester County is not intended to portray its complete history. It can only scan the happenings of its almost 340 years, many of which have never been put into pictures. It is my hope that this effort will be a unique contribution to what others have done in recording the county's past and a stimulus to a dedicated historian to undertake the complete history which has been contemplated since the early days of Dr. William Carter Stubbs but not yet accomplished.

To achieve some cohesiveness I have abandoned chronology at times and placed many pictures according to their relationships. I hope my readers will not be disturbed if they find some of their pictures placed out of timing. It has also been imprudent and sometimes impossible to identify all places, people, and dates.

Caroline Baytop Sinclair

Acknowledgments

In undertaking this book I had many misgivings, but was reassured by the support of the Gloucester Chamber of Commerce and the Peninsula Trust Bank, and by Bernard L. Walton, a native of Gloucester and also the project director of Donning Publishers. These have been encouraging and supportive throughout the project and I wish to give special thanks to Mr. Downey, president of the Chamber, Mr. William Farinholt, president of the Bank and Miss Betsy Bobbitt, Donning Company's pictorial coordinator.

My great appreciation is extended to Mrs. Harry Corr who has worked with me constantly in innumerable ways; to Miss Elsa Cooke, editor of the *Gazette-Journal*, who has extended to Mrs. Corr and me the use of her facilities, files, and advice; to her father, the eminent John Warren Cooke, who has graciously expressed his interest and kindly agreed to write the introduction; to the Gloucester Historical Committee and its chairperson, Miss Margaret Lamberth, for granting us office space in the Debtor's Prison and full use of the Committee's files; to the *Daily Press* and its staff member, Mrs. Joan Marble, who has opened the picture files in the Gloucester office to Mrs. Corr and me.

I also wish to acknowledge the help of Mrs. Clementine Bowman who has read and criticized my manuscript; I requested this favor because of her vast knowledge of county affairs over the last three decades and especially during my recent years of absence from the county; I am very grateful. Mrs. Corr and Miss and Mr. Cooke have been most helpful in providing supplementary information.

I acknowledge with gratitude the skill and generosity of Mrs. Ben B. Manchester who typed and edited for me from my own defective typescript and in doing so kept a remarkable time schedule.

My appreciation is extended to all those who gave information by letter, interview, newspaper clipping, or phone calls and to the kind friends who offered encouragement, transportation and hospitality when I was working on this project in Gloucester.

The production of this book has had its disappointments and its frustrations but it has also been challenging and exciting. I have become even more appreciative of my home county, its beauties, its achievements and its people.

Caroline Baytop Sinclair

Cow Creek Mill was still grinding grain — and selling groceries too! Melvin Hogge drives the delivery truck. Courtesy of Mrs. Melvin R. Hogge

Introduction

Gloucester's Past in Pictures, a volume of illustrations and text describing phases of Gloucester County's history, will be of large interest to natives, and other longtime inhabitants and those who have been part of the great migration of recent years. The constant flow of new residents into all sections of the county attests to the area's appeal.

Caroline Baytop Sinclair has written this work which should hold the reader's attention from beginning to end. Dr. Sinclair, a county native whose family roots go far back, is a highly qualified historian. The organizations responsible for the publication were fortunate in obtaining her services.

Gloucester County has been an agreeable place to live during the three and one-half centuries of its existence. In common with this entire blessed part of Tidewater there have been unhappy periods but in most respects the times have been good to the county and its people. This book gives tangible evidence of that fact. All persons interested in Gloucester County's general welfare can hope that the familiar slogan, "Land of the life worth living," will still be used in the years ahead to describe the county.

John Warren Cooke
July 16, 1991

Mount Prodigal may have been built by the Hubbards (Dabney, P. 421) but it was the home of Charles Roane when it was vandalized by Bacon's men in 1676 and for many, many years thereafter it was owned by the Roanes. From the hill on which Mount Prodigal stands a sloping vista extends across a wandering stream to Route 17 near Adner. Courtesy of the Gloucester Historical Committee; photo by Bob Bailey

CHAPTER ONE
The Colonial Period: 1607-1776

Nearly every farm in Gloucester County has had its collection of arrowheads, pipestems, an occasional mortar and pestle, a spearhead or a tomahawk. Some of these stone objects date to hundreds and even thousands of years before the English came to America. Some of the arrowheads are made of stone which must have been brought from far away. There has never been an intensive and sustained study of Gloucester's Indians and much that the colonists learned about them has been unrecorded.

The Indians whom the English found at Kecoughtan (Hampton), at Jamestown, and in Gloucester, were friendly, though wary. Although Powhatan, the great chief of many tribes, had a number of homes there is certainty that some of them were on the north side of the York River. The site at which Pocahontas saved Captain John Smith's life has been variously placed at Purton, Rosewell, Shelly, and Powhatan's Chimney; it is generally agreed that it did occur on the bank of the York River in Gloucester County. Indeed Pocahontas should be considered a child of Gloucester though most of her service to our budding nation occurred in and around Jamestown. The Indians of the area were friendly or hostile depending on the circumstances of the time as they served successively under Powhatan and Opecancanough. Cruel and treacherous at times, nevertheless Powhatan, through Pocahontas and his own ministrations, was responsible for the survival of the settlers through the devastating "starving time" at Jamestown, so both Pocahontas and Powhatan

This statue of Pocahontas, erected at Jamestown, enables us to imagine the young Indian maiden running lightly through the woods. Courtesy of the Association for the Preservation of Virginia Antiquities

can be remembered as persons who contributed to our history. Pocahontas died in England and was buried at Gravesend on March 21, 1617. Powhatan survived her by just a year. When the Indian massacre occurred in Gloucester in 1646 there had been hostilities in Virginia for several years.

Gloucester is a thrice burned out county. Its parish records were destroyed at the time of Bacon's Rebellion (1676); the clerk's office was successfully entered by an arsonist (1820); during the War between the States the existing records were sent to Richmond for safe keeping and lost or destroyed when Richmond was burned (1865). The records remaining have been painstakingly collected or made available by students and researchers over the years. County records from 1865 have been carefully maintained by the long tenured clerks among whom were Alexander Wiatt, Basil Bernard Roane and Charles King.

A comprehensive history of Gloucester County has not yet been written but throughout its three and one-half centuries of existence Gloucester's history has been recorded in the memories of its citizens and sometimes by pen, paint, and camera. It is this heritage peculiar to this old Tidewater county which we intend to preserve in this book of photographs and limited print.

Gloucester County was created from York County (then Charles River County) in 1651. Gloucester was divided into four parishes of the Anglican Church (then the official church of this English colony), Abingdon, Ware, Petsworth, and Kingston. Churches were built in each parish, vestries were formed and rectors were brought over from England or sent there to be ordained. In this period most functions later relegated to county officers were performed by the vestries and tithes (taxes) were collected and expended by them. In 1791, at the request of its petitioning citizens, Kingston Parish was separated from Gloucester and became Mathews County. With the "disestablishment" of the Anglican Church in 1776 tithes were no longer collected for the support of the churches. The parish lines became the boundaries of the county districts and so remained for many years. In 1971 the number of districts was increased to five in order to balance the populations more evenly. The new districts were called York and Gloucester Point and the governing Board of Supervisors was increased from three to five.

Although Gloucester lost most of its Chesapeake Bay frontage to Mathews in 1791 it still has an extensive shore line for it stretches along five rivers—York, Severn, Ware, North, and Piankatank and encompasses both sides of two of them. Although settlement was forbidden on the north side of the York River after the Indian massacre of 1644, land had been granted there previously and no doubt homes had been established. Hugh Gwyn applied for a land patent in 1635 but it was not granted; the first known grants were to Robert Throckmorton in 1635, to George Menefie in 1639 and to Augustine Warner and John Robins in 1642. The Menefie grant soon passed to John Mann and thence to his daughter, Mary Page. These early grantees and their descendants have been associated with the leadership and progress of Gloucester County and Virginia since colonial days.

Just where and when Gloucester's first court house was built remains unknown, but it was before 1676 and tradition places it at Elmington gate. In that year eight people were killed by Indians "near Gloucester Court House" and a little later, in the same year, Nathaniel Bacon "harangued the people in front of Gloucester Court House." This early building was replaced soon after 1680 when Edmund Gwyn deeded six acres of land to the county "for the building of a Court House, prison and other necessary buildings and conveniences." A new brick Court House was built in Gloucester shortly before 1684. That this building was in the present court house area but not within the Green has been established by careful documentary and archaeological evidence. (Sinclair and Lewis). The Court House within the walled Green has been dated 1766 and was built on land advertised for sale that year. A fragmentary plat, dated 1769, shows a court house on one-half acre of land. Two new prisons were built in 1769. Gloucester's Historic District is centered by five brick buildings within a brick wall and enhanced by the Confederate Monument and the nearby Botetourt Building. It was built by John Fox, Jr., as a tavern prior to the Revolution.

In the early eighteenth century Gloucester became prosperous with a number of large self-sustaining plantations, a healthy seafood industry and the shipping of tobacco, timber, and other products to northern ports and England. Tobacco warehouses were established and some of the planters maintained their own docks and barges or other boats for shipping. Gloucester Point was first named Tyndall's Point for an early explorer and mapmaker; the colonists built a fort here in 1667. This fort was strengthened and rebuilt several times. Extensive fortifications were established during the Revolution. An hour after the

Captain John Smith was among the colonists who came to Jamestown in 1607. He was strong, capable, and energetic and he assumed the leadership of the colony after it fell into dire straits. He was able to deal with the Indians to procure food and, though taken prisoner and threatened with death, he survived. Pocahontas is believed to have saved his life and certainly she became his friend and that of the other Englishmen. She brought food to them in "the starving times" and enjoined a period of peace with Powhatan's tribes. Smith insisted that all the colonists labor to provide food, shelter and safety for the colony and gradually his efforts earned some degree of independence and stability was achieved. In October of 1608, Captain Smith was severely injured by an explosion of gunpowder. In order to secure medical attention he returned to England. It was there years later that he saw Pocahontas again. Courtesy of the Association for the Preservation of Virginia Antiquities

surrender at Yorktown, British troops, under Lieutenant Colonel Tarleton, surrendered to the French Brigadier General deChoisy on October 19, 1781, as ordered by General Washington.

Gloucester Town was planned in 1680 and laid out at Gloucester Point in 1707 and a thriving port developed, rivaling Yorktown across the river. A young Virginia lady visiting in Philadelphia about this time wrote home about Philadelphia's growth and that "the shops are almost as good as those in Yorktown."

With its extensive waterways Gloucester County had easy access to Williamsburg and Baltimore, the more northern ports, and England. The colonists prospered, schools and churches were developed; sons were sent to William and Mary and, sometimes, to Princeton or abroad, most often to England. Tutors were engaged and occasionally a governess was brought to teach the girls. Music, dancing, and needlework were considered essential skills, and the girls were taught how to manage the large households and extend hospitality to the many guests. Gloucester is and always has been a welcoming haven for visitors. Many of the most prominent families in Virginia had early homes in Gloucester—the Lees at Paradise, the Washingtons at Highgate, the Warners and Lewises at Warner Hall, the Whitings at Elmington, the Robins at Point Lookout and Level Green, and many others. In the eighteenth century most of these homes were built near the water with a large acreage, sweeping lawns, and many dependencies. The plantation owners depended upon tobacco for their wealth; indeed it was used as money, but it was exhausting to the fields. Thus new ground was cleared for the money crop and many hands were required for the clearing and for the planting and tending of the crops. Gloucester had a large black population; few of these were free. The slaves who worked in the house and yard were usually housed nearby; the field hands had cabins in the slave quarters which were erected in small communities on the various farms.

Gloucester, is, and always has been, a rural community. There have always been small homes along the rivers where the owners supplemented their

In return for the courtesies and honors extended him in the King's name Powhatan sent his highly decorated deerskin mantle as a present to King James of England. Courtesy of the Association for the Preservation of Virginia Antiquities

income as fishermen, crabbers, and oystermen by tending small crops, a pig or two and, perhaps, a cow. The section known as Guinea, located between York and Severn Rivers, had a stable population of watermen in the colonial period. These families, of British origin, retained their indigenous speech and customs into the twentieth century when good roads and schools brought many new people and modern conveniences into the waterbound area. The origin of its name remains an unsolved mystery.

Gloucester has a wealth of colonial homes still standing, most of them, quite naturally, have been altered extensively over the years. The county is especially blessed with the homes dating to the seventeenth century which retain many of their original and interesting architectural features. Two notable in even early days were Marlfield in Petsworth Parish and Poropotank (also known as Chelsea and Violet Bank), owned by the Buckners and Booths, respectively. They suffered destruction from fire and/or weather but pictures of them survive (p.26).

Gloucester gave shelter and a never-found burying place to Nathaniel Bacon in 1676. Although most Gloucester citizens were loyal to the Crown and resentful of Cromwell, the desire for freedom from oppression and for independence was strong in Gloucester and in 1776 its men and women were ready to stake their lives and fortunes to win it.

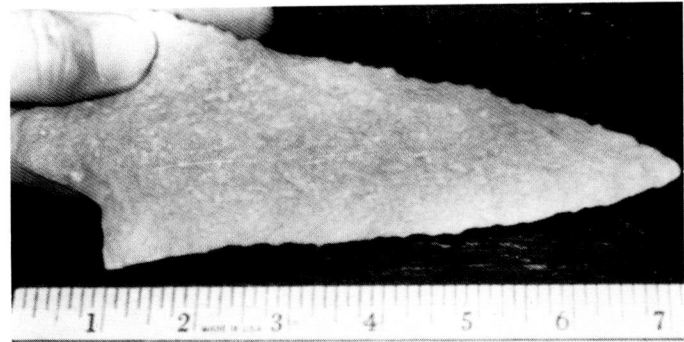

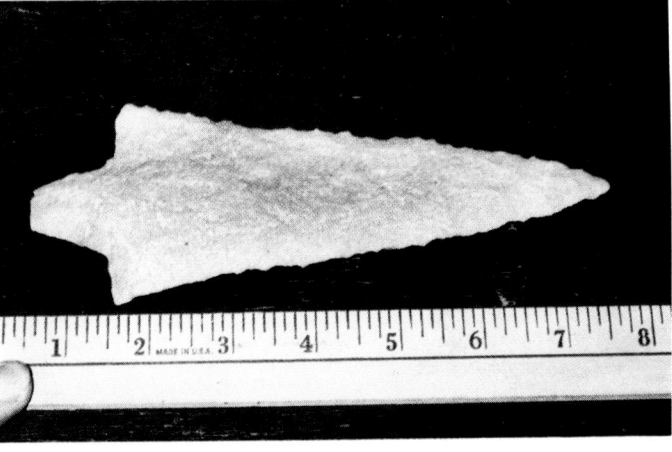

These large Indian artifacts, two beautifully shaped spearheads, and one massive axehead were found on Timberneck Farm. Courtesy of John W.C. Cablett, Jr.; photos by Jean Corr

PETITION OF JOHN ROLFE FOR PERMISSION TO MARRY POCAHONTAS
MS. Ashmolean 830, Fol. 118, 19. Bodleian Library, Oxford. Exact Size

[Extract]

Lett therefore this my well advised protestacion, which here I make betweene God and my owne conscience be a sufficient wytnes, at the dreadful Day of Judgement (when the secretts of all men's hartes shal be opened) to condemne me herein yf my chiefe intent & purpose be not to stryve with all my power of boddy and mynde in the undertakinge of soe waighty a matter (noe waye leade soe farr foorth as man's weaknes may permytt, with the unbridled desire of carnall affection) for the goode of the plantacion, the honoure of oure countrye, for the glorye of God for myne owne salvacion, and for the convertinge to the true knowledge of God and Jesus Chryst an unbelievinge creature, namely, Pokahuntas—to whome my hart and best thoughte are and have byn a longe time so intangled & inthralled in soe intricate a laborinth, that I was even awearied to unwynde my selfe thereout. But Almighty God who never faileth those that truely invocate His holy name, hathe * * * * *

At your command most willinge to be desposed.

JO. ROLFE.

Presented to the Pocahontas Memorial Association by David Bushnell, Esq.   Copyrighted by Pocahontas Memorial Association

Petition of John Rolfe for permission to marry Pocahontas

This picture, taken from the portraits of Pocahontas and her son, Thomas Rolfe, is in King's Lynn Museum, Norfolk, England. It is more natural and more appealing than those usually shown. Truly a child of the woods and waters of Gloucester she was taken to Jamestown by the colonists and there, with her father's consent, married John Rolfe. In 1616, with her husband and son, she went to England where she was received as royalty. She also renewed her friendship with Captain John Smith. She became ill and died just before she was to return to Virginia. Courtesy of the Association for the Preservation of Virginia Antiquities

General Thomas Mathews was born in Saint Kitt, grew up in Norfolk, Virginia, and became an officer and brigadier general in the Revolutionary Forces and militia. After the war he was a member of the Virginia legislature and Speaker of the House. In gratitude for his support of their petition to become a separate county, the people of Kingston Parish named their new county for him. His portrait, from which this photograph was made, hangs in Mathews Court House. Courtesy of the Gloucester-Mathews Gazette-Journal

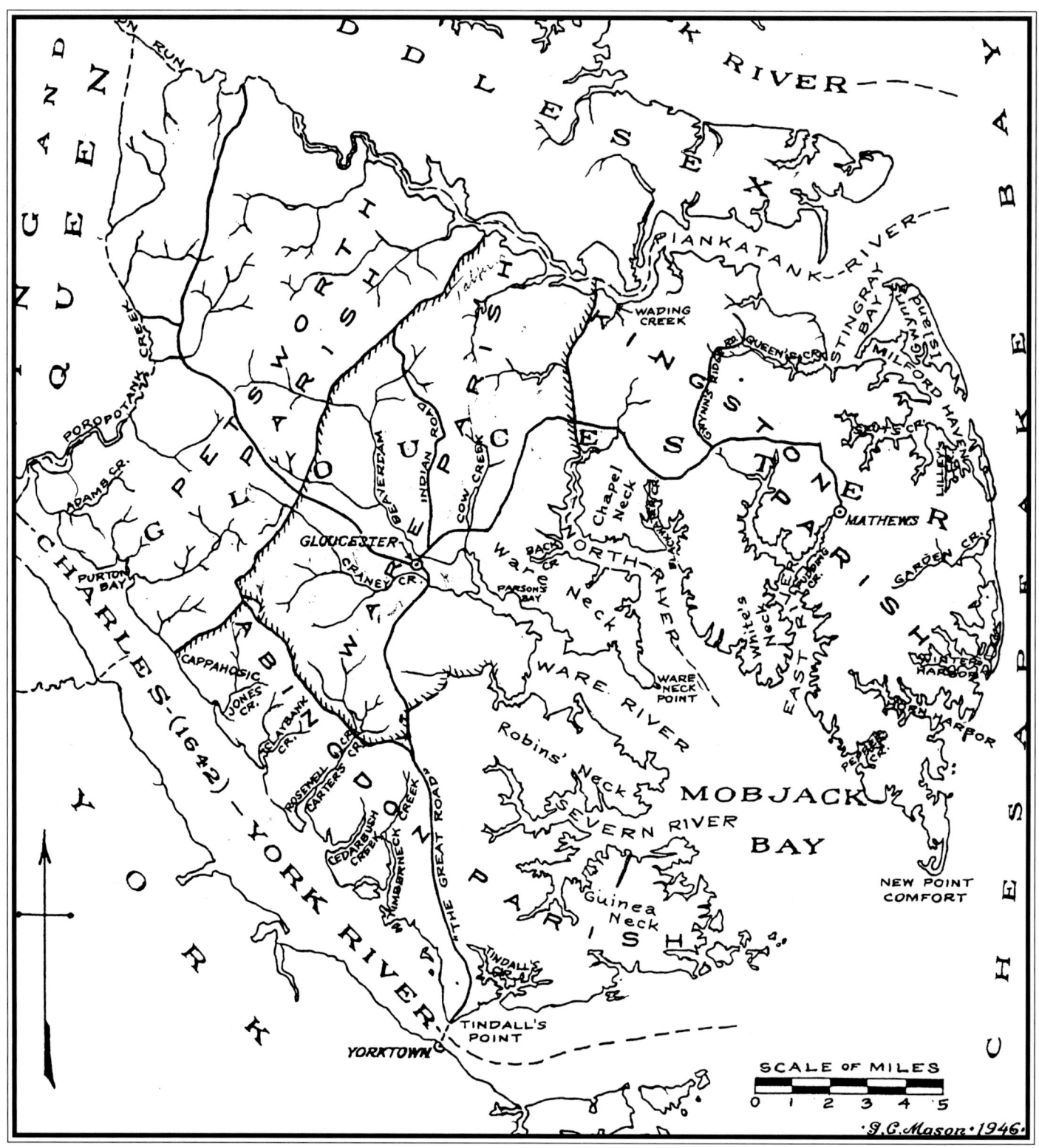

This map of colonial Gloucester County shows clearly the lines of the four original parishes: Kingston Parish became Mathews County in 1790/1791. The parish lines remaining in Gloucester became the boundaries of the three voting districts of the county and remained virtually unchanged until 1971. The two colonial churches, Abingdon and Ware, which are still standing in the county, have exteriors which are almost identical with those of the original structures. (p. 182)

Warner Hall was erected by Augustine Warner I soon after 1642 on a large patent granted in that year. In these pictures the east wing is believed to be the original house. The west wing is an eighteenth-century addition which still stands. The large central portion, built by John Lewis in the eighteenth century, was burned in 1849 and rebuilt in 1905 as what Virginia Landmarks described "as a grand architectural gesture." The east wing burned in recent years and has been restored by the present owners. In the top picture the Severn River can be seen beyond the front lawn. The trees formerly graced this area in great variety and abundance. Warner Hall was the home of the Warner-Lewis family for nearly two hundred years. The graveyard is owned and maintained by the APVA. Warner Hall is listed in both the Virginia and National Registers of Historic Landmarks. Warner Hall was occupied by Bacon and his men who carried off supplies and other articles in 1676. Courtesy of the Sinclair Family and Jean Corr

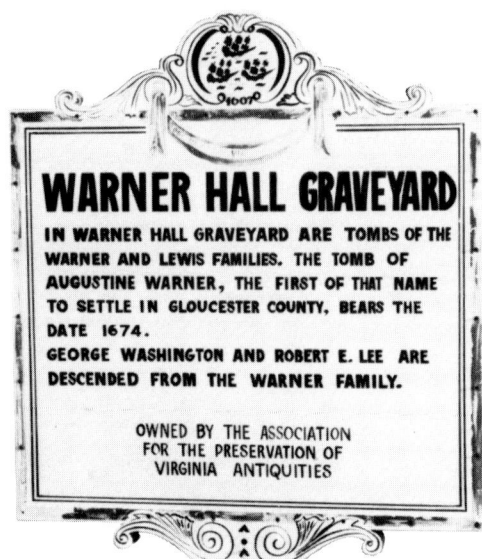

Historic marker

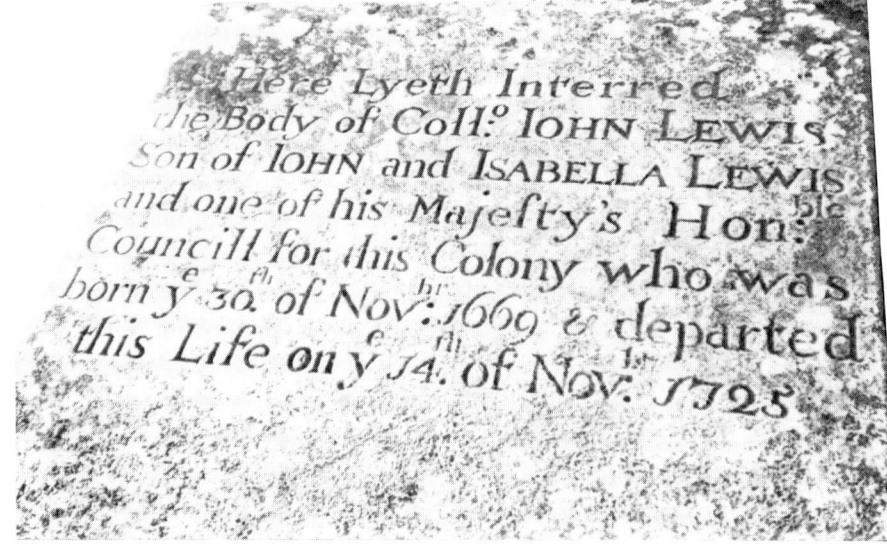

Gravestone

19

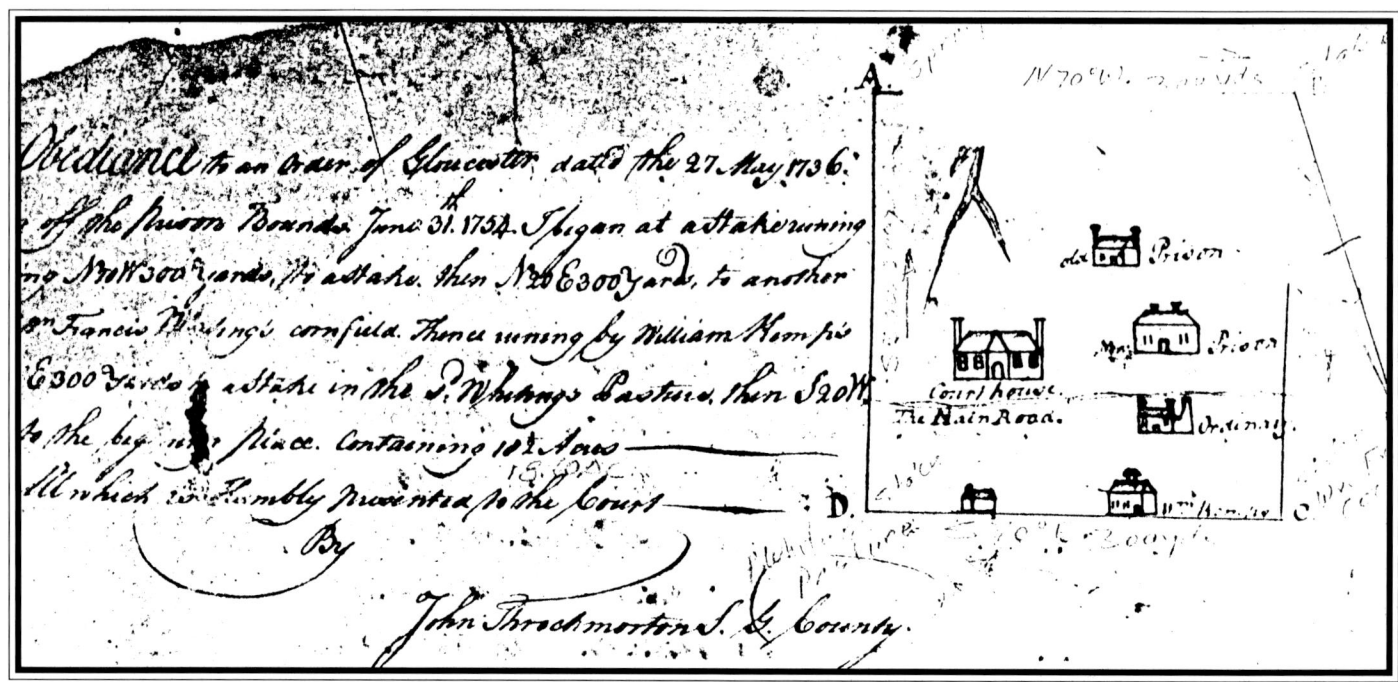

Plat of 1754. Courtesy Gloucester County Records

These three plats showing Gloucester Court House and dated, respectively, 1754, 1769, and 1774 reveal, in sequence, something of the origin of the colonial court house which is still in limited use. The earliest of these is the evidence on which the claim of the date, 1754, was given for the Debtor's Prison. This was proved wrong by archaeological investigation (Report of A. E. Kendrew, architect, 1978, filed with the Board of Supervisors and the Gloucester Historical and Bicentennial Committee). This plat and that of 1769 survived the fire of 1820 in fragmentary form and can be found in the county records. The plat of 1774 is a plan proposed by John Fox, Jr., for the town to be known as Botetourt. The notes and dates relate also to happenings of the time. This plat, believed to be published here for the first time indicates the location of the court house built on Gwyn property about 1682 and also other buildings of that era. It is published with permission of the Huntington Library from which this copy was obtained by the author.

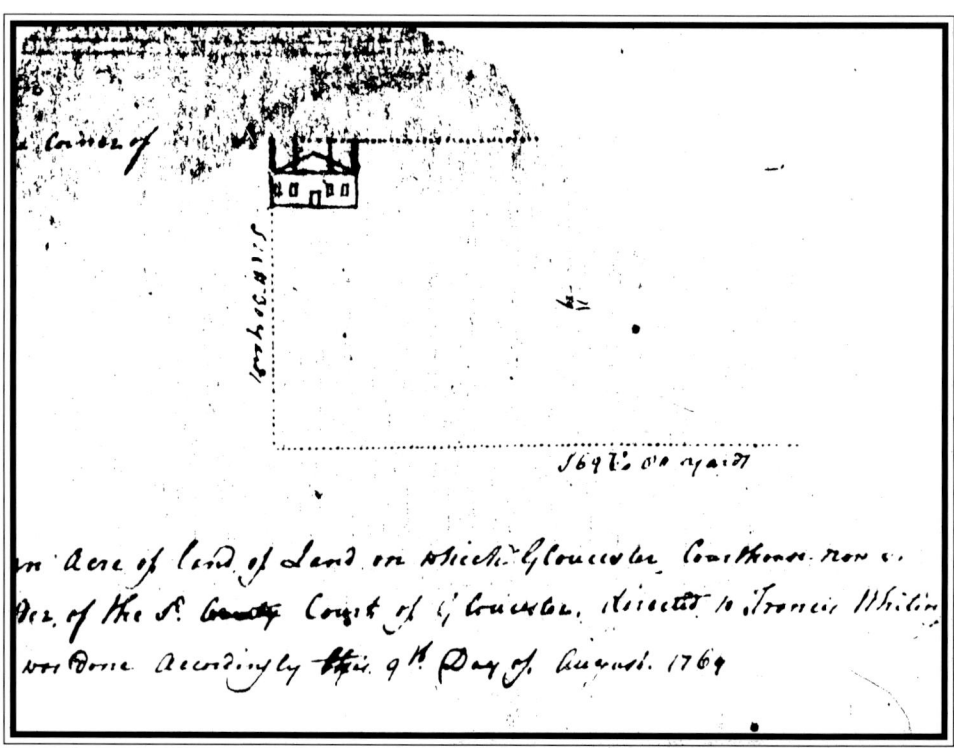

Plat of 1769. Courtesy Gloucester County Records

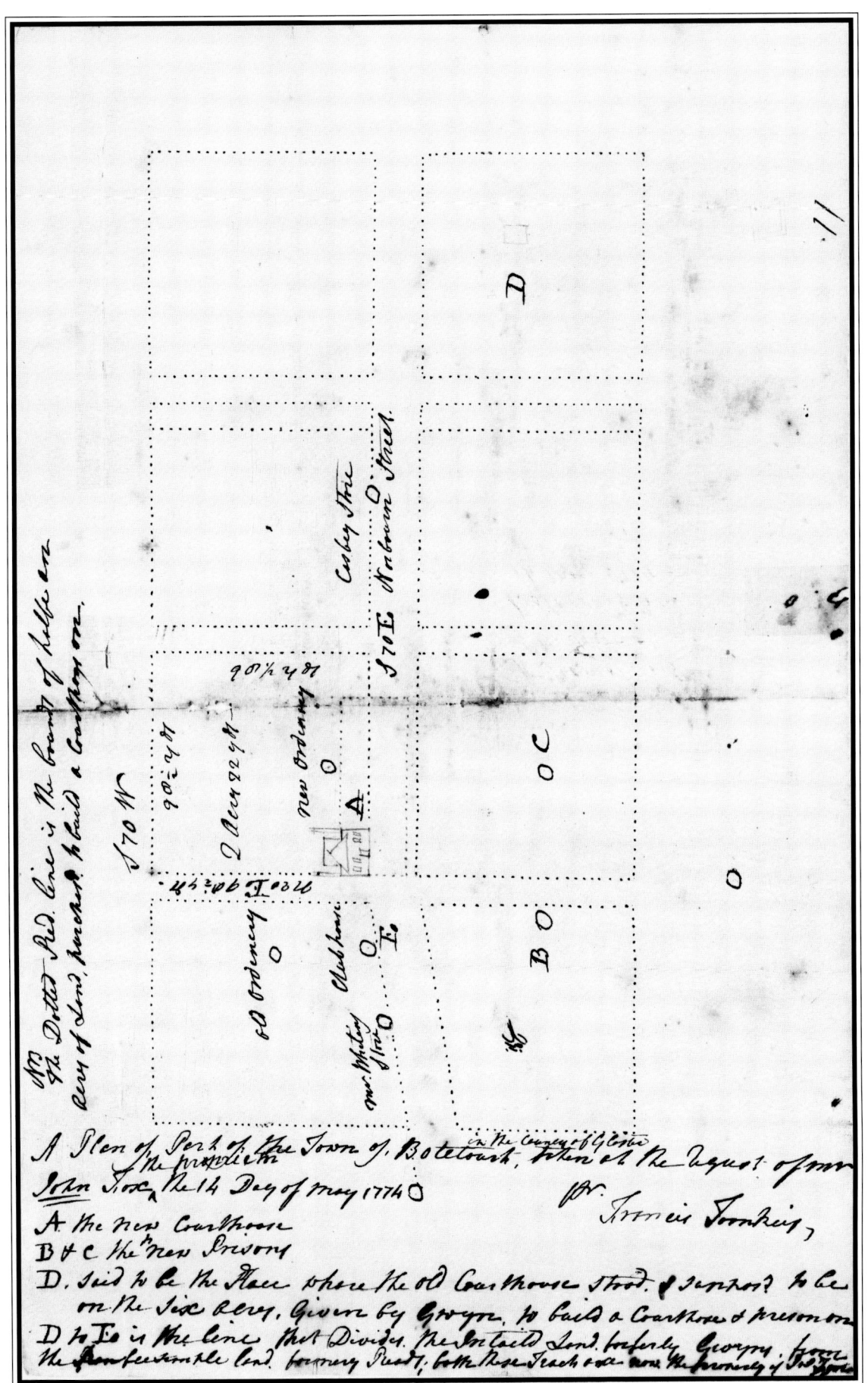

Plat of 1774. Courtesy of Caroline Sinclair with permission of the Huntington Library.

This large building, known as Botetourt Tavern, was unusual for a rural area in the eighteenth century. It is believed to have been built by John Fox, Jr., prior to 1769 as a first move toward the town which he planned to develop around the new court house. It remained a tavern or hotel, recently owned and operated by the Cox-Lawson family who closed it about 1935. In 1965 it was bought and restored by the county and became the Botetourt Administration Building in Gloucester County. Courtesy of the Gloucester-Mathews Gazette-Journal

The monument pictured is not in Gloucester and was erected by order of Congress in 1883. Other scenes here were taken before 1893. The date of the Court House is now believed to be earlier—in 1766. Edge Hill Ordinary is now the Woman's Club Building and is usually called Long Bridge Ordinary. Might the building at the upper right be an altered Botetourt Building? Scenes at Gloucester Court House, shown clockwise from the left are: York Monument, Yorktown, Va.; Old town Court House, built 1793; two scenes on Court Day; Edge Hill, an Ordinary Inn of Colonial Days; center photo—Street in Gloucester Court House before the Fire of 1893. Courtesy of the Sinclair Family

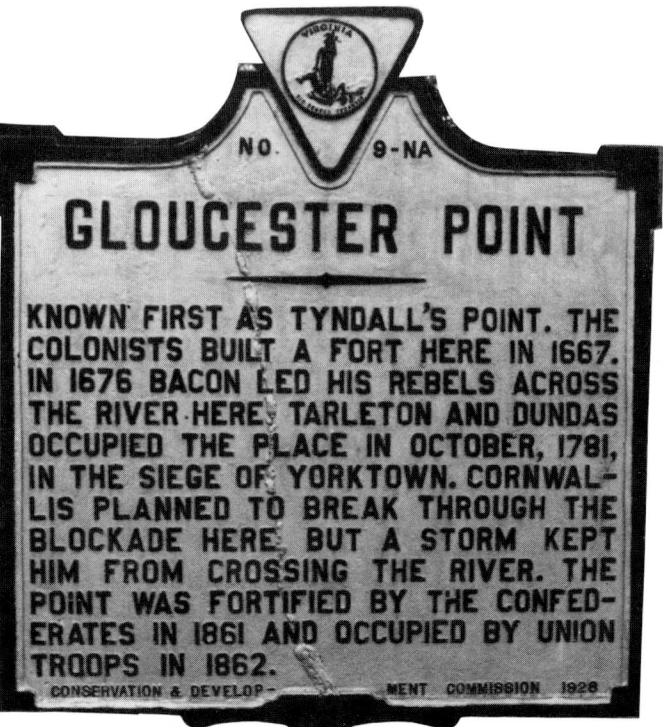

These two markers are evidence of the early growth and significance of the area now known as Gloucester Point. When the county was told to erect a port there fifty acres were laid off. This is the land which now provides the county with a thriving waterfront park. Courtesy of R. Edward Brown

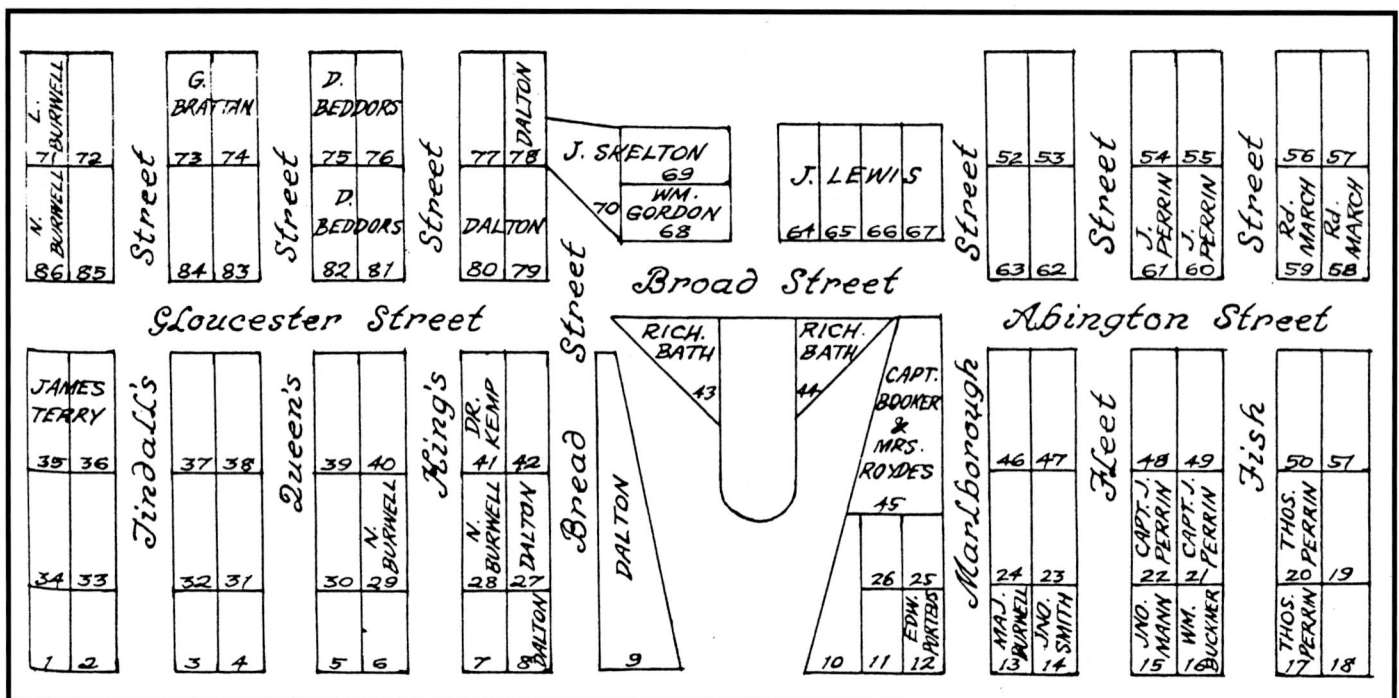

(Top map) In 1707 Gloucester Town was laid out and surveyed by Miles Cary. It was already a thriving port with deep water, large vessels, and a warehouse for storing and processing tobacco and other commodities. Original plat in Gloucester County Records Taken from Mason, Polly Cary, Vol. 2 p. 53.

(Bottom painting) The view of Gloucester Town shows many houses on the high banks of the York, a fort at the left end and probable fortifications above the fort. Little remained of Gloucester Town after it was taken over by the British troops during the Revolution and after it suffered fire from both sides during the final battle. Courtesy of the Gloucester Historical Committee; photo by the Mariner's Museum

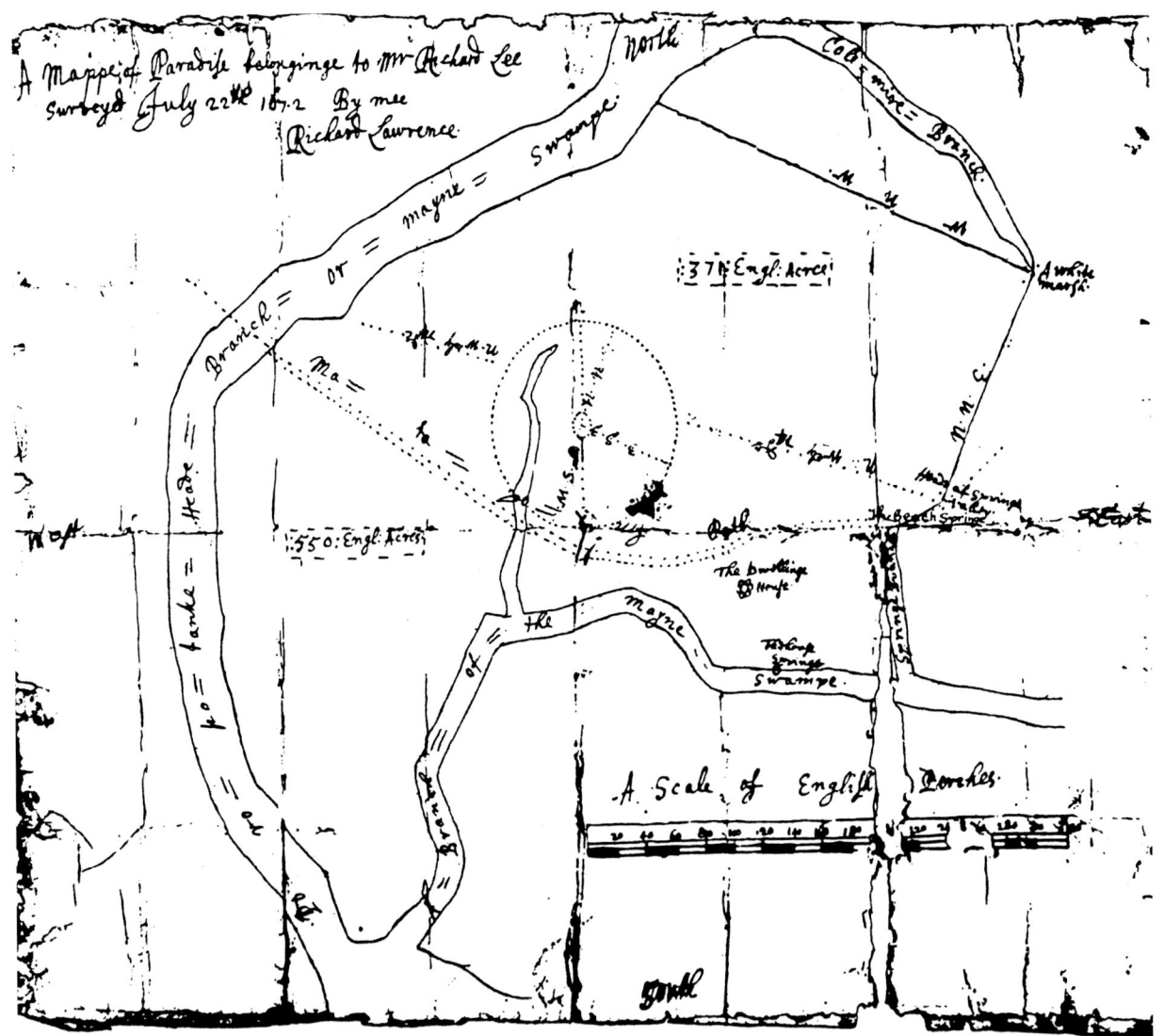

Paradise was one of the earliest Lee homes in America, and was situated near the head of Poropotank Creek, in the western section of Gloucester County. Colonel Lee's "Dwelling House" is shown by the plat to have stood on the south side of the historic "Mattapony Path," a section of which has survived as a woods road crossing Poropotank Creek west of this plat. The "Branch of the Mayne Swampe" depicted on the plat was the "Bridge Branch," named for nearby Toms' Bridge, which crossed this branch just east of this plat, at the foot of the hill on which later stood the building known as Toms' Hill School. Across this bridge once ran the main north-and-south county highway, variously described in early records as "the Rappahannock Road Path" or "the Main Road to the Dragon Bridge"; this was long since relocated a half-mile further east, to straighten out the hard-surface road. The plat's historical value is enhanced by its having been surveyed by Richard Lawrence, the man who, five years later, faced by immediate execution as a ringleader in the unsuccessful Bacon's Rebellion, rode off into the snowy forest and was never seen or heard of afterward. The original plat is in the Alderman Library, Charlottesville. Comments are quoted from Mason, Polly Cary Records of Colonial Gloucester County, Vol. II, Frontispiece.

These next pictures show the fine architecture of the period. John Buckner of Marlfield brought the first printing press to Virginia but it was banned by Lord Culpeper, then governor. Poropotank was built by George Booth and is probably of the very early eighteenth century; it is on Poropotank Creek and was antedated by a tobacco rolling house (warehouse) also on the creek. The Booths occupied the home for four generations. Courtesy of The Daily Press *and Elizabeth R. Gray*

26

Cappahosic House: the marker gives the location and early history. Long associated with the Stubbs and Baytop (see clipping from 1869 below) families this property has had an absentee owner in recent years. Its history and fine architectural features merit proper restoration.

Courtesy of the Gloucester Historical Committee; photo by Bob Bailey

Q 10A
CAPPAHOSIC

SEVEN AND ONE-HALF MILES SOUTHWEST IS CAPPAHOSIC, WHERE A FERRY WAS ESTABLISHED EARLY IN THE EIGHTEENTH CENTURY. ON THE OLD CHARTS, THIS INDIAN DISTRICT LAY BETWEEN WEROWOCOMOCO AND TIMBERNECK CREEK. POWHATAN IS SAID TO HAVE OFFERED IT TO CAPT. JOHN SMITH FOR "TWO GREAT GUNS AND A GRINDSTONE". JOHN STUBBS PATENTED THE CAPPAHOSIC TRACT IN 1652 AND 1702 AND A FEW YEARS LATER BUILT "CAPPAHOSIC HOUSE", WHICH HAS CLIPPED GABLES AND INSIDE CHIMNEYS WITH EIGHT UNIQUE CORNER FIREPLACES.

Courtesy R. Edward Brown

Private Entertainment

BY T. C. BAYTOP,

AT CAPPAHOSIC, GLOUCESTER COUNTY, VA.,

On York River

Being also the only Licensed Agent for the sale of Land in the County, I am prepared to accompany parties wishing to purchase or lease.

There are between 30 and 40 Farms on hand, of various areas and prices, from $8 to $35 per acres. Many of these Farms could be sub-divided to great advantage. They are mostly immediately on one of the five rivers of the County, affording good water fronts, with fine fish and oysters.

I have also a very extensive tract of land covered with white-oak and chestnut, suitable for railroad ties. Steamers Admiral and Kennebec leave Richmond and Baltimore daily,

mar13-4t   Address GLOUCESTER COUNTY HOUSE

From *Baltimore Episcopal Methodist* (newspaper), Saturday, March 27, 1869.

Toddsbury, built by Thomas Todd about 1650, consisted of two large rooms and a Jacobean porch. It was twice enlarged in the eighteenth century and has beautiful paneling and other features of that period (p. 198). Courtesy of the Sinclair Family

Lowland Cottage was built about 1670 and was the home of Robert Bristow, a loyalist whose land was escheated when he went to England and remained there. This picture was taken for a booklet published in 1969. It has long been the residence of the Taliaferros and their descendants. It is beautifully located on the Ware River. Lowland Cottage is on both the Virginia and National Registers of Historic Places. Like most of the seventeenth century homes it has a low roof with dormer windows which may have been added. Courtesy of the Gloucester Historical Committee; photo by Bob Marble

Abingdon Glebe was built for the Abingdon rector in 1674 but it is and was then in Ware Parish. It was confiscated by the state in 1802 and since that time has been used as a laymen's residence. It is a recognized Virginia and National Landmark and retains features of seventeenth and early-eighteenth-century architecture. The recent owners placed it in the protective custody of the Association for the Preservation of Virginia Antiquities (APVA). Courtesy of the Gloucester Historical Committee

The Free School House, on a branch of the Severn River, was willed in 1675 by Henry Peasley to found a free school "for the children of Abingdon and Ware parishes forever." The school became one of the first four free schools in Virginia and was said to be the best of the four. After a few years the school was moved to the Abingdon Glebe and the Peasley property of more than six hundred acres was sold. The money secured was used to support public or free education in Gloucester until it was contributed to the erection of the Kenney Building at Botetourt in 1925. In this early Peasley home the brick walls of the first floor are original and other features are thought to be. Ancient foundations of an annex and other structures have been found in the yard. A school was again held in this house after the Civil War and prior to the beginning of the public schools in 1871. Courtesy of the Gloucester Historical Committee

Known as the "Warehouse" this residence has been uninhabited for many years; the date of erection is unknown but interior features identify it as mid-eighteenth century or earlier. It overlooks Warehouse Landing which is now a popular recreation site, but in colonial days it was a much-used shipping port. Tradition says that a load of intended wives arrived there from England in the sixteen hundreds. Courtesy of the Gloucester Historical Committee; photo by Bob Bailey

This plaque honoring Nathaniel Bacon is on the wall of Gloucester's Colonial Court House. A visitor from Colonial Williamsburg once expressed some surprise when he saw this commemorative tablet. He remarked that he had thought Bacon was considered a rebel and by many a traitor. Most certainly this was never so in Gloucester. In this county many rallied to his cause and when he was stricken with illness and death his remains were protected from the devastation intended by his enemies. To this day the site of his burial is unknown. Courtesy of the Gloucester Historical Committee

The Gloucester Token is believed to be the first coin minted in this country. In 1974, in preparation for the Bicentennial, a replica of the coin of 1714 was issued by the Gloucester Historical Committee. This issue, photographed here, lacked one "i" in Virginia. This error was corrected in the next issue. Only two originals of the coin are known to exist. The better known is in the Numismatic Collection of Johns Hopkins University The second was found in Gloucester and sold in California. This more recently discovered token has revealed lettering not formerly discernible in the other, indicating further research is advisable. Courtesy of the Gloucester Historical Society

As troops left Gwyn's Island, John New entertained them with food and drink at the commodious Botetourt Tavern, Gloucester. It was built circa 1769 and owned by John Fox, Jr., the intended developer of Botetourt Town. This building is now owned by the county and houses office and meeting rooms. It has been restored by the county and is an excellent example of mid-eighteenth century architecture. Courtesy of the Gloucester Historical Committee

CHAPTER TWO
Revolution and Independence
1776-1808

When John Page, first president of the Virginia Council and acting governor of Virginia because of Patrick Henry's illness, received John Hancock's letter telling of the signing of the Declaration of Independence, it was already sixteen days old. Gloucester, like much of Virginia, had made preparations for this event.

John Page, Lieutenant-Governor, to John Hancock, President of Congress.
(From Manuscript Letter in Library of Congress.)

In Council W^{ms}burg July 20, 1776.

Sir
We had the honour to receive your Letter of the 8th Instant inclosing the Declaration of Independence and the Resolve of Congress respecting the Augmentation of the Rifle Corps at New York-
We shall take care to have the Declaration immediately published so as that the People may be universally informed of it, who, we have the pleasure to inform you, have been impatiently expecting it and will receive it with Joy.
We are perfectly satisfied of the Utility of Riflemen and wish it were in our Power to assist in raising the number but the Convention has adjourned and we are vested with no Powers, which can in any manner inforce or carry into execution that Vote; If Commissions could be sent to proper Persons they might raise Companies which would have a Right to march to New York, but we could not oblige them to do so.
It is with Pleasure, Sir, we observe that you say in consequence of the Declaration you are fully convinced that our affairs may take a more favorable turn, and we firmly rely on the Protection, and Continuance of the powerful Interposition, of that Being, whose Power no Creature is able to resist. I have the honour to be with the greatest Respect.
Sir
Your most obed^t & most hble Servt
JOHN PAGE Pt

33

Reacting in opposition to a succession of oppressive acts of Parliament, beginning with the Stamp Act in 1765, Gloucester's desire for independence was strong. It had been nurtured by Lewis Burwell and Thomas Whiting as Burgesses and members of the Virginia Conventions, and by the leadership of John Page of Rosewell, who was in a decision making position for the colony, the Commonwealth of Virginia and the newly formed nation from 1773 until his death in 1808.

John Page of North End also served on the Kings Council and as a Burgess. He was on the committee that drafted the memorials sent to George III from Virginia after a meeting in Williamsburg, April 16, 1678, in response to the Townshend Act.

Lewis Burwell II (1769-1779) and Thomas Whiting (1775-1776) were members of the House of Burgesses and represented Gloucester in the five Virginia Conventions. Lewis Burwell was active until his death in 1779 (Burwell, George H. *Record of the Burwell Family*, p. 8).

Thomas Whiting served the cause of independence in a variety of ways but most notably as Chief Commissioner of the Virginia Naval Board. Gloucester, like other Tidewater counties, was extremely vulnerable because of its six rivers and frontage on the Bay. Her waters were open to the marauding British. Gloucester County contributed heavily to the Virginia Boats (Navy) through its shipyards, shipwrights, and seamen. Privately owned ships and small boats were used for the protection of the colonists and also to run past the blockades and bring in supplies and ammunition.

On April 1, 1774, Governor Dunmore sent the British Marines to take powder from the Powder Horn in Williamsburg. The Gloucester County Committee of Safety met to condemn and protest the action officially four days later.

On July 14 of the same year, the inhabitants of Gloucester were summoned to the Court House and the Gloucester Resolutions were passed.

On November 7, the Committees of York and Gloucester authorized a "Tea Party" in the York River in defense of Virginia's boycott of the importation of British goods.

When on March 2, 1775, Thomas Whiting and Lewis Burwell were elected to the Second Virginia Convention as Gloucester's representatives, it was evident that the transition from a colony of Britain to an independent government had been accepted and that a degree of stability had been attained. The county continued to send these same men to the five Virginia Conventions of the revolutionary period.

Not all of Gloucester's people were for independence. A few left for England at the beginning of dissension. Others maintained their loyalty to the Crown while deploring the acts of Parliament and some of these departed when war became inevitable. Legend, rather than documentation, has identified loyalists

John Page of Rosewell (1743-1808), later governor of Virginia, served in that capacity in 1776 because of Patrick Henry's illness. This painting was done in Philadelphia when Page attended the First Continental Congress. Page represented the First District of Virginia which, of course, included Gloucester. Courtesy of Cecil W. Page

who remained. A few were prosecuted and some lands were escheated.

On September 13, 1775, the Gloucester Militia was organized at Gloucester Court House. By order of the Committee of Safety, officers were nominated as follows: Sir John Peyton, colonel; Thomas Whiting, lt. colonel; Warner Lewis, county lieutenant; and Thomas Boswell, major. Sixteen captains, sixteen lieutenants, and sixteen ensigns (only thirteen listed) were also nominated (*Virginia Gazette*, October 21, 1775).

In April of 1775 and several times thereafter the Gloucester Committee of Safety requested that regiments and militia from Gloucester be retained in the county for its protection, but these requests were seldom heeded. Consequently, Gloucester's men were widely scattered and the county remained vulnerable.

From Williamsburg, on May 26, General Andrew Lewis reported that fifty ships were sailing up the Piankatank River. Seeking supplies and recruits, Governor Dunmore hoped to improve the health of the men on his ships by camping in the rural area.

The Seventh Regiment under Colonel Dangerfield was immediately marched to the mainland across from Gwynn's Island. They were joined by Gloucester Militia and later by other troops. Batteries were erected and ammunition was supplied. On July 9, at eight in the morning, the attack began on Dunmore's fleet and his camp. The *Otter* and the *Dunmore* were damaged and fled to open sea. When a crossing was achieved the British were found to have fled, leaving dead and dying behind, many of them Negroes. Disease had taken its toll. Dunmore's defeat at Gwynn's Island resulted in his departure from Virginia and return to England. General Lewis and some of his men remained at Gwynn's Island until October, collecting stores and salvaging ships. Samuel Eddins of Gloucester constructed a machine with which he swept the Piankatank and recovered seventeen anchors and cables for the Virginia Navy. As the men left Gwynn's Island they were greeted and fed by John New, then the proprietor of Botetourt Tavern at Gloucester Court House.

After Gwynn's Island no major battle was fought in Gloucester until 1781, but there were skirmishes and much harassment along her roads and rivers.

Although there was a lull in the enemy's naval activities after Lord Dunmore's departure, British ships returned to Chesapeake Bay and its tributaries in 1777 and continued activities there so that Gloucester's people and properties were in constant danger. During these years most of her men were away and her militia at home were depleted in health, number, and ammunition. Nevertheless Gloucester was ordered to supply troops—and did— though

Rosewell never attained its former grandeur after the Revolutionary War, and the Pages never really lived there again. John had neither means nor the desire to restore the plantation because of his concern for and involvement in the affairs of the new nation. Rosewell was sold after his death and devolved to the Booth, Catlett, and Deans families. It burned in 1916 and remains as a magnificent and historic ruin. Rosewell, usually considered the most magnificent of Virginia's colonial homes, was built on Page property (originally a part of Timberneck and owned by the Manns). Mann Page I started the mansion in 1725. After his death in 1730 construction was continued by his wife and his son Mann II who had a large family and was the father of John Page of the Revolution. Courtesy of Katherine Lewis Pickett

John Page, John Peyton, Thomas Whiting, and other leaders pled that her men were needed at home to protect her waterways. They were also necessary to supply the food needed for her own army and to counter the raids of the enemy who were constantly carrying away her stock, her grain, and her servants. The militia was called out all too frequently.

Gloucester's contribution to Virginia's naval action has not been well recorded but it is known that she furnished ships and many experienced seamen. A few of the captains, some of them employing their own ships and crews are known—Captains Thomas Lilly, Robert Tomkies, Edward Hughes, and Peter Bernard.

Although the Gloucester Committee of Safety was one of the first to be formed and was very active, a complete listing has never been made. It was said to have at least twenty-three members (Ryan, p. 21). The names of Warner Lewis, Jasper Clayton, John Peyton, Matthew Fontaine Maury, John Curtis, and Phillip Tabb (not certain, Ryan, p. 21) have been discovered from several sources. John Page (Rosewell) was a member of the Virginia Committee of Safety. This was a very powerful body which, according to David Mays (David J. J. Mays, ed., *The Letters and Papers of Edmund Pendleton to Richard Henry Lee*, Vol. 1., p. 132) could "wield almost dictatorial power over both the sword and purse of the colony." Gloucester County had been victimized during most of the war. Small boats were sent to the shores of her rivers and creeks from the British ships which stood guard in the Chesapeake and Mobjack bays. In 1780, Benedict Arnold headed a raiding party which looted and burned the Page home on North River and probably others.

Because of her well-stocked farms, wooded areas, many rivers and fertile fields, Gloucester was a source of food and other commodities for both armies.

When in October of 1781, the French ships appeared off the Virginia coast, Lawrence Hobday of Gloucester was one of the pilots who brought them into the York River.

When Cornwallis decided to make his stand at Yorktown he immediately built strong fortifications on the Gloucester side of the York, both to secure control of the river and to provide a way of escape should his troops become trapped on the south side. These fortifications were manned by cavalry under the command of Colonels Simcoe and Tarleton and under the general command of Colonel Thomas Dundas. Washington countered by sending French troops and Gloucester Militia to several posts along the Great Road (now approximately Route 17). The British raids into the county were terminated at the Hook when the French, under the Duke deLauzan, supported by the

Fairfield on Carters Creek (the home was often called Carters Creek) was built by Lewis Burwell II in 1694 to replace an earlier home built by his father. Lewis Burwell II died in 1779. His wife, Judith Page Burwell, and her younger children moved in with her brother at Rosewell. She died in 1780. The Burwells never returned to Fairfield. It was sold and burned before 1902. There is no house on the property now, but it has been declared a Virginia and National Landmark. It is noted for the importance of the two Lewis Burwells and for the architecture of the building. Courtesy of the Gloucester Historical Committee

Gloucester Militia, defeated Tarleton's command. Tarleton withdrew to his encampment at Gloucester Point and there the British remained until the surrender on October 19, 1781. In the Battle of the Hook, the militia, commanded by General Weedon, were minimally supplied with arms and ammunition and depleted by long service and the ravages of war. John Dixon of Airville and his men of the Light Horse Cavalry also supported at the Hook. Dixon's cavalry unit supplied their own horses and arms and served before and during the Yorktown campaign.

In 1781, Thomas Jefferson estimated that there were 850 men in Gloucester's Militia; how many served in this unit during the war no one knows. Some of these men were also enlisted in the Virginia regiments and in the Continental Lines. If Gloucester's Militia had 850 men in 1781 an examination of Lewis's roster (Lewis, Elizabeth Dutton, *Revolutionary War Roster*) would support that about 1,800 Gloucester men were enrolled in the colonies' defense during the war, more than 309, the total estimated for Virginia by Ryan (note that in the estimate of 1,800 some may have been counted twice).

When Cornwallis deemed his situation in Yorktown to be desperate, he planned to send his men across the York on October 16 in order to escape to the north through Gloucester. Their small boats were driven ashore by a sudden severe storm but the French troops and the Gloucester Militia stood guard just beyond the fortifications at Gloucester Point. A British soldier surmised that the British would never have got through their lines (Popp as reported by Ryan, p. 88). The storm was good fortune for both sides, no doubt, saving many lives.

A surrender was arranged. It occurred in Yorktown at two o'clock in the afternoon on October 19, 1981, and an hour later at Gloucester Point (then Gloucester Town). Cornwallis did not appear and Washington retired to his quarters, having directed General Lincoln to receive the sword offered by General O'Hare, acting for Lord Cornwallis. Across the river, at three o'clock, the British troops marched out in surrender and Lt. Colonel Tarleton's sword was received by General deChoisy.

The surrenders on the two sides of the York River, in Yorktown and Gloucester, are generally considered to have terminated the War of Independence though the Treaty of Paris was not signed until 1783. In Gloucester after the surrender the war still seemed ever present. Gloucester Town was shattered. Few homes remained and shops, the tobacco warehouse, and shipping facilities were badly damaged. Little England is the only pre-revolutionary home in the area which survives to this day, perhaps because owners of that time were believed to be loyalists. The French troops remaining assisted in rebuilding homes. The women and children from Yorktown and the British sick and wounded had been brought to Gloucester where a hospital had been established. After the surrender the sick and wounded remained and also the doctors

This well-known portrait by Joshua Reynolds of Lord Dunmore (the Fourth Earl of Dunmore), the last of the English governors of Virginia, was displayed at the Victory Center in Yorktown. Copies have appeared elsewhere and in several publications. The Battle of Gwyns Island and early involvement at Gloucester Point (then Gloucester Town) brought the War of Independence to the Gloucester residents from the very beginning. From the collection of the Scottish National Gallery

and staff; militia were ordered to guard them. The French army remained in Gloucester. The British and French impinged heavily on food and other necessities already in short supply. In November there were still 1,387 British in Gloucester, six hundred of them too ill to move. Some remained until the spring of 1782 and French troops stayed until July 1 of that year. (Ryan, p. 91).

Many of the large landowners had given of their wealth and found themselves heavily in debt; fields were no longer productive because of neglect and times were hard. Sir John Peyton, the appointed sheriff, whose duty it was to collect the taxes, found so many people unable to pay that he became personally indebted for the delinquent taxes. This indebtedness was passed on to Peyton's successors, John Dixon and John Fox, Jr., according to the laws of the days. Some of the French depredations were submitted as claims and paid for by General Rochambeau. Sir John Peyton claimed starvation among Gloucester people in 1786 (Ryan, P. 97), but Gloucester citizens helped each other, both in the war and in the peace that followed (Ryan, pp. 98-100). At least two county buildings, the Botetourt Tavern, two colonial churches (Ware and Abingdon), two or more ordinaries, and many homes survived the war and most are still standing today. As the militia and other troops were released they returned to their homes and began to bring their lives, their families and their properties into order. They reveled in peace and in the newly won independence.

The portrait from which this photograph of General George Washington was made, hangs at Mount Vernon. Washington knew Gloucester well, having visited relatives here from boyhood. He was a nephew of John Washington of Highgate and a kinsman of the Lewis family at Warner Hall. Courtesy of the Mount Vernon Ladies Association and the Founders Society

It was General Lafayette who advised Washington that as many of Gloucester's men as possible should be kept in the county for its protection as Cornwallis approached Yorktown and began to re-fortify Gloucester Point. Thus the Gloucester Militia and others under General Weedon were able to join French troops and defeat Tarleton at the Hook.

Their continued entrapment of the British forces in Gloucester was an important factor in concluding the Battle of Yorktown and bringing about the surrender on the two sides of the York River. Courtesy of the Gloucester -Matthews Gazette-Journal

Seawells (pronounced Sow-ells) Ordinary was built and operated prior to 1737. Horses were raced there and George Washington is said to have participated. It was headquarters for the Gloucester Militia during the war and their arms were often stored there between engagements. Lafayette is known to have stayed at the Ordinary and probably Washington also. No doubt important conferences were held at this old ordinary. This building has been a residence, a store, and in this century has again become a popular restaurant and meeting place. It has been moved from its proximity to Route 17 and restored to its eighteenth century appearance; most of the building is believed to be original. Courtesy of the Gloucester Historical Committee; photo by Bob Bailey

TARLETON'S LAST FIGHT

HERE, AT THE HOOK, TARLETON, COMMANDING THE CAVALRY OF CORNWALLIS'S ARMY, FOUGHT AN ACTION WITH CHOISY'S FRENCH FORCE AND VIRGINIA MILITIA, OCTOBER 3, 1781. THE DUKE DE LAUZUN'S CAVALRY CHARGED TARLETON, WHO RETIRED TO GLOUCESTER POINT. THERE HE WAS BLOCKADED BY THE FRENCH AND BY VIRGINIA MILITIA.

IN ETERNAL MEMORY
OF THE FALLEN MEMBERS OF THE
DUKE DE LAUZUN'S HUSSÁRS
LED BY THE DUKE AND COUNT JOHN POLERECZKY
OF HUNGARY AGAINST COLONEL TARLETON AND
THE BRITISH CAVALRY AT GLOUCESTER HIGH, VIRGINIA
IN THE MONTH OF SEPTEMBER 1781
ERECTED BY
COUNT PULACKI & DUKE DE LAUZUN LEGIONS

The roadside marker of The Hook and the Memorial Plaque to the Hussars of the Duke De Lauzun tell their own stories. Courtesy of E. D. Brown

Point Lookout is the early Robins home on the original Robins tract, still called Robins Neck. It was granted in 1642 and John Robins built a home there before 1644. The present house has been dated architecturally as 1714. It is believed to have been built on the original foundations by a grandson of the immigrant. The Robins family lived there until after the Civil War. When R.C. Selden owned it he added a full second story and large attic over the original story-and-a-half and English basement. Courtesy of the Sinclair Family

General Rochambeau, commander of French forces at Yorktown, was endeared to Gloucester people because of his leadership and loyalty during the Revolutionary War and because of his help to the area after the surrender. Courtesy of the Gloucester-Mathews Gazette-Journal

Little England was built on the shore of Sarahs Creek by Thomas Perrin in 1650. The place is sometimes called Sarahs Creek. It survives as a magnificent structure with fine brickwork and paneling, in a gracious setting and with a beautiful view of the York River. Appropriately a portion of the 1981 Bicentennial celebration was held on these grounds. Courtesy of the Gloucester-Mathews Gazette-Journal

Masonic Building. Botetourt Lodge No. 7 is one of the oldest Masonic lodges in the country. The lodge dates to 1757 (chartered by Fredericksburg Lodge) and 1773 (English charter) when the present name was adopted. The Virginia charter was received in 1785. This building was occupied before 1886. It is located just off the Court House Green. Courtesy of R. Edward Brown

John Clayton, the noted botanist, was clerk of court here for more than fifty years. Gloucester has commemorated him with a tree on the Green, planted by the Garden Club of Gloucester, by naming the first clerk's office for him, and by creating the John Clayton Natural History Society. Mathews maintains a nature trail and aspects of his home, Windsor, in his honor. Foreign countries extol his name as a naturalist. The finest exhibit of his work is said to be in Sweden. Clayton's extraordinary contributions have received renewed attention in this century. Courtesy of R. Edward Brown

The John Clayton Building has been called the "mystery building" because the date and occasion of its building are unknown, nor is it recorded that John Clayton ever used it. This early clerk's office was burned by an arsonist in 1820 and rebuilt on the remaining foundations and walls. Photo by Jean Corr

41

Robins Mill was on original Robins property (1642) and was built and operating prior to the Revolution. It is referred to in the War records, sometimes as Dixons Mill. Here the mill is running—the windows are wide open—and Archibald Robins, the owner, is taking a rest after feeding his dog. Mr. Robins died in 1927. The operation of the mill was continued but the mill house was burned in the early 1940s. The house on the hill overlooking the property and known as The Mill is still owned by Mr. Robins' great-grandchildren. Courtesy of Georgiana Sinclair Cumming

CHAPTER THREE
"Before the War"
1800 - 1861

As an old county of a young country there was much to be done. Thomas Whiting and Lewis Burwell did not survive the Revolution and able successors had to be elected. An ardent patriot, John Page spent most of his time in Richmond, Philadelphia, and New York helping to form the new nation. In Gloucester, with Warner Lewis, he helped to bring Abingdon Church to stability and to establish the Episcopal church in Virginia and the nation. In the county private schools were established for boys and girls and sometimes plantation schools for the blacks. Some of the owners had their slaves baptized and given religious instruction. Tutors and governesses were brought to the plantations and shared with the children of nearby homes. This practice was continued into the twentieth century.

The Court House became a gathering place and the economic and political center for the men of the county; the exchange of news and products occurred there. On Court Day, held once a month, buggies and wagons crowded the court house area and horses were tied to every available railing. For many years it was considered inappropriate for women and girls to appear in the village on Court Day.

It was not customary for Gloucester families to sell their "people" but if on rare occasions this was done it was on a Court Day and, according to tradition, at the Honey-pod Tree.

In its struggle back to a reasonable prosperity Gloucester lost some of its population and some of its early families. Large estates were divided and redivided to accommodate the many heirs and, in some cases, were sold. Large families like the Pages of Rosewell and the Lewises of Warner Hall were widely scattered. Whole families moved south or west. Farming, now more diversified, again prospered. Life in Gloucester became much like it had been in colonial days except that the people now made their own decisions and elected their own leaders. There was another difference; slavery was no longer the accepted way of life for both black and white. The industrial north and the agricultural south gradually came to differ on the subject of slavery especially with reference to the new states coming into the union. Virginia's farms were not so large nor as productive as previously. Money was scarce but the sea and the land provided food in abundance and life in Gloucester still had a cavalier quality when war came again.

In 1812 Gloucester's men again responded; again it was her long waterfront which was most vulnerable. A roster of the men involved has not been compiled but it is known that the Gloucester Militia was called out often while British ships were in the vicinity in 1813 and 1814. Some of the captains under whom they served were William Rogers, Hugh Gwyn, Thomas Hall, Catesby Jones, John B. Seawell, Richard Jones, and James Baytop (Stubbs, *The History of Two Virginia Families*, pp. 133, 134, and 137). Captain John Sinclair of the Revolution, having moved from Isle of Wight to Gloucester, engaged his several ships in patrolling the Mobjack Bay and its rivers. He was successful in damaging and sending to flight a British schooner which had ventured into the Piantatank. (Lanciano, p. 270) While Sinclair was at sea the Militia was three times ordered to assemble on the shores of his home in Robins Neck. On January 25, 1814, the orders read: "You will immediately convene your company at Capt. Sinclair's and on your arrival there you will take steps to have every man about brought to your quarters. No man able to walk must be permitted to remain at home. . . .Seven sails are now in sight" (Stubbs A *History of Two Virginia Families*, p. 133). It was probably on this occasion that Captain Sinclair's two sons, John and Jefferson, joined the Militia. The younger was so small that a forked stick was placed in the ground to help him hold his gun (Sinclair, *Stories of Old Gloucester*, p. 30-32).

This early picture of Court Day at Gloucester Court House was probably taken circa 1906-1911. Courtesy of Elizabeth Harwood

Some historians have considered the War of 1812 a draw. When Britain withdrew her ships and troops America celebrated a victory even though the enemy had looted and burned Washington and never admitted defeat (Treaty of Ghent 1814). Britain withdrew to defend against European threats and to avoid dividing her military resources. Since England agreed to restore properties taken, the United States claimed a diplomatic victory.

While Virginia statesmen considered alternatives to slavery, manufacturing and other ways of building a new economy, Gloucester continued to depend upon agriculture, forestry, and seafood for the livelihood of her people, both white and black. Schools were started and prospered, sometimes under the sponsorship of or by private individuals. Much instruction was given by family members and by philanthropic volunteers. Public schools were not started in the county until 1871 (Gray, p. 137).

Roadwork was infrequent and at times even the main roads were almost impassable. Oxen were used for heavy hauling, mules were raised for fieldwork and horses were bred for work, for transportation and for sport.

Gloucester people visited freely and were always known for their hospitality. Those who went to Hampton and Baltimore traveled by boat; those who lived on the rivers used their boats for local visiting. Riding and boating were social accomplishments. Horse racing, popular in the period, survived as a casual sport; tournaments, a form of jousting, were held; and fox hunting was popular with both men and women. Gloucester has always been a county in which horses were treasured and bred for quality, sport, and love as well as for utility and profit.

Religious life in the county continued to expand in the nineteenth century. Four Protestant faiths were established in the county and had built churches here before 1900. Petsworth Episcopal Church did not survive the loss of tithes and the devastation of war but after some years of struggle both Ware and Abingdon survived and have had active parishes for more than three hundred years.

Baptists were active in the county before the Disestablishment and built their first church in 1790. It was in Petsworth District and was named for the district. Closed in 1852, the site has since been known as Meeting House Corner. The first minister and probable founder was Robert Hudgins. Although

The Honey-pod Tree is remembered because it stood for years in the middle of the road as one approached the Court House from the east. For many years it was surrounded by a fence. When the tree was finally taken down to make improvements to the road an excavation revealed a British sword but no signs of a coffin. Tradition held that Nathaniel Bacon or his stone-filled coffin had been buried there. In recent years the Honey-pod Tree has been best memorialized as the title of Thomas Calhoun Walker's autobiography. This picture is taken from an old post card. Courtesy of the Gloucester-Mathews Gazette-Journal

Sherwood (known as Cloverfields and, later, as Shabby Hall) is on the Ware River. Captain John Sinclair enlarged these holdings to include Four Point Marsh and homes and properties later known as Greenway, Marlfield, Lands End, and Bay Cottage. John Sinclair sold Sherwood to Robert Colgate Selden before the Civil War. The Selden family lived there for more than a hundred years. Courtesy of the Sinclair Family

Severnby and Eagle Point were both built on property originally a part of Warner Hall. Eagle Point served as home for the Bryan family both before and after the Civil War. It was built by John Lewis of Warner Hall in the late eighteenth century. Courtesy of the Sinclair Family

its life was relatively short, the Baptist faith is strong in Gloucester today. Seven churches, all active in 1936, Union, Beach Grove, Ebenezer, Providence, Newington, Beulah, and a second Petsworth, were all missions of or developed from the first church at Meeting House Corner.

In colonial Virginia when all of the churches were Anglican many of the black people were baptized in and attended those churches and many continued to do this, but after slavery ended the blacks built and supported their own churches. From the first most of them embraced the faith of the Baptist Church.

When the first Petsworth Baptist was closed and many of its people moved to Ebenezer it served both black and white in large numbers. A membership of 1,057 was reported, of which it is written that only fifty-seven were white (Gray, p. 113). By 1936 there were eighteen Baptist churches with black congregations scattered throughout the county. Most of these are still active. There are now at least twenty-one Baptist churches in the county.

Gloucester County was visited often by Francis Asbury, the first Methodist bishop in America. He and other Methodists had services in Abingdon Church and other buildings soon after the Revolution. In the early 1900s there were eleven Methodist churches spread throughout the county. The earliest of these, Bellamy and Mount Zion, were built in 1795. Joseph Bellamy gave the land and is considered the founder of the church which bears his name. An early minister was James Baytop, formerly a vestryman and strong supporter of Petsworth Episcopal which did not survive the Revolution and "disestablishment." Bellamy and most of the other early Methodist churches are still strong in the county today.

The first Presbyterian church was organized in the Court House area in 1881 after extensive study by the Home Mission Committee of East Hanover Presbytery. Land for the church was given by Mr. and Mrs. George Hughes. This church, a frame building, was started in 1929 and officially dedicated in 1940; to this extensive additions were made in 1956 and 1980. This has served as a community center because of its willingness to welcome many groups there because of its location. Early in the twentieth century when transportation was still difficult, an afternoon Sunday school was held there in which several denominations combined. Many community meetings have been held at Gloucester First Presbyterian and several community services have emanated from there.

During the ministry of the Reverend William Groves two other Presbyterian churches were built in Gloucester County, Severn in Robins Neck at Naxera and Groves Memorial in Saddlers Neck.

These four denominations: Episcopal, Baptist, Methodist, and Presbyterian, dominated the religious life of Gloucester County well into the twentieth century. A Catholic church was built in the Court House area in 1939. Since that time other denominations have established churches in the county.

By 1861 many Virginians and some of the people of Gloucester had come to believe that slavery was wrong but many of them saw it as an economic issue rather than a moral issue. And always there were the questions: If the slaves are freed how will we work the farms? And how will the blacks earn a living? Who will take care of the old and the sick? These questions had certainly not been answered when South Carolina seceded on December 20, 1860. Gloucester had just confirmed her allegiance to the Union for the Gloucester Militia, at their last meeting of 1860 had decided to erect a monument at Yorktown. This was done on October 19, 1861 with the following inscription:

> Erected October 19th, 1860 *to mark the spot of the surrender of Lord Cornwallis, October 17th, 1781, by the officers of the 21st Regiment Virginia Militia and Companies of Gloucester.*

This monument stood as the sole commemorator of the surrender until the more elaborate one was commissioned by Congress and erected in 1883. Not until 1981 was a commemorative marker placed at the surrender site in Gloucester.

Goshen

White Hall

Riverside

Residence Rowland Clark

Cow Creek Mill was built by Marius Vernon Kerns in 1866. Its water-turned wheel turned to grind corn and wheat well into this century. In later years the building has been a roller skating rink and an antique shop. This large building still looms above the mill pond and above Route 14. Courtesy of Charles J. Kerns

Two of these four homes, pictured prior to 1906, Goshen and White Hall, are pre-Revolution homes built by the Tomkins and Willis families. Rowland Clark, an artist of considerable talent and skill, married the daughter of Captain Byrd and later moved to New York. Dr. Rose, of Norfolk, moved to Riverside, which he called Kilravock, in 1901 shortly after his marriage to Jane Parks. He died here in 1942. Courtesy of the Sinclair Family

Wind, water and tide were used as sources of power. Marius V. Kerns, a millwright of the mid-nineteenth century, built six mills in Gloucester County. Courtesy of Charles J. Kerns

This well at Sherwood was a type found on many Gloucester farms before electricity was in common use. Courtesy of Donald R. Perritt

48

This smokehouse at Camden is typical of those found on many of the larger plantations of the early days. It is built of brick with a peaked roof and covered opening. The meat was cured, smoked, and stored here. Courtesy of the Gloucester Historical Committee

Early Ferry: The Hampton Rhodes area and the Middle Peninsula are now joined by the Coleman Bridge. Until the late twentieth century transportation across the York and other rivers was by ferry and the early ferries were boats powered by men with oars. Later they were motor driven. Men and horses were frequent passengers. If the boats were not big enough the horses might swim alongside. This picture were taken about 1890. Courtesy of Donald R. Perritt

The Reverend William Byrd Lee served as rector of Ware Church from 1881 to 1921. He became rector of Abingdon also in 1885 and served both churches with devotion and distinction until his retirement in 1921. A home was built for Mr. and Mrs. Lee because of the devotion of the people and because they wished the Lees to remain in Gloucester. There have been many faithful and beloved ministers in Gloucester, but because of his long tenure, his loving nature, his strong faith, and his broad ministry, Mr. Lee will be long remembered. His youngest daughter, Eliza, still lives at the home, Leeland. Mr. Lee died in 1931.
Courtesy of Abingdon Episcopal Church

The first Baptist church in Gloucester was built in 1790 but one of the oldest to offer continuous services is Union at Achilles which claims its origin as 1801. Union grew under devoted ministers and with an increasing congregation until the War Between the States when services were discontinued. Most of the men of the church joined the Confederate services. The pastor, Rev. William E. Wiatt, was the chaplain of the First Virginia Infantry. He resumed the pastorate at Union and served until 1871. The building pictured is presumed to be that built or enlarged in 1884. The history of Union Baptist was published in 1976. This publication pictures the larger and more modern church now in existence.
Courtesy of Sandra P. Hogge

Newington Baptist Church was first a branch of Ebenezer and became a separate church in 1873. The original building was replaced by a handsome brick structure which has had several additions over the years. Newington is near the Court House Village. It was served in earlier days by three long-term ministers, the Reverend William E. Wiatt, the Reverend R. A. Folkes, and the Reverend Harry L. Corr. *Courtesy of the Gloucester-Mathews Gazette-Journal*

Providence Baptist Church, Ordinary, showing only a portion of the church and several men from Newington on a visit about 1938. *Courtesy of Mrs. Melvin R. Hogge*

Ebenezer Baptist Church. Ebenezer conducted a baptismal service at Burgh Westra on the North River, August 1927. *Courtesy of Mrs. Melvin R. Hogge*

Zion Poplars Baptist Church, Gloucester, is traditionally a church for black people. After the Civil War many of the blacks organized their own churches. With a strong religious faith they have built and maintained these. These churches have been an important factor in stability and progress of the county over the years. *Courtesy of the Gloucester-Mathews Gazette-Journal*

51

St. Paul's Baptist Church has served a black congregation since 1890. It is on route 629, not far from Roanes. Courtesy of the Gloucester-Mathews Gazette-Journal

Shepherdsville Baptist Church, Ark, Va., established 1884. Courtesy of Mrs. Catherine King

Gleaning Baptist Church, Harcum, Va., established 1893. Courtesy of Mrs. Catherine King

Bellamy and Mt. Zion Methodist Churches were both built in 1795. The land for Bellamy was given by Joseph Bellamy, the founder and an early minister of the church. The first building burned in 1831 and was replaced by one of brick (1833) pictured here. A larger brick building was constructed in 1930. The older building was used as a museum but has now been converted for other purposes. Note the well-kept cemetery to the left. Courtesy of the Gloucester-Mathews Gazette-Journal

Mt. Zion Methodist Church is on a hill overlooking Route 14. The church was founded in 1795 by Mrs. Mary Mason Tabb of Toddsbury. It was closed for a number of years and revived by the efforts of The Reverend D. G. C. Butts and a new building was erected in 1907. Courtesy of the Gloucester-Mathews Gazette-Journal

Bethlehem Methodist Church originated in 1789 but the church, in lower Gloucester, was not erected until 1808. A second church was built in 1870 and it was remodeled in 1908. Courtesy of Myrtle M. Rexrode

Singleton Methodist Church in Ware Neck was derived from Bellamy in 1844. When Memorial Church was no longer used it was added to Singleton in 1933 and now houses a large congregation. Courtesy of the Daily Press

The First Presbyterian Church was established in 1888 near the Court House. The land was given by Mr. and Mrs. George Hughes. The frame building was replaced by one of brick in 1929-1938. The church was active in the community during this period but the building was not dedicated until 1940. This church, pictured here, was opened for a variety of community services and at one time housed a community Sunday School. An education building was completed in 1964 and a new sanctuary and other additions were constructed in 1980. Courtesy of the Gloucester-Mathews Gazette-Journal

Severn Presbyterian Church at Naxera in Robins Neck was established in 1884 with a membership of twenty. Services were held in a one-room schoolhouse until the first church building was completed in 1892. The present structure was designed and built by Mr. Samuel E. Sterling, an elder of the church. It was dedicated December 7, 1922. The wing to house the educational program was added in 1956. Photo and information are from the program in commemoration of the ninety-first anniversary of the church, July 20, 1975.

The Monument of the Surrender, Yorktown, pictured here resulted from efforts of the Gloucester Militia following their last muster at Gloucester Court House in May 1860. On that occasion the officers, decrying the long delay of Congress in properly marking the surrender site, took up a collection and made plans for this monument. The inscription was: Erected October 19th 1860 to mark the spot of the surrender of Lord Cornwallis, October 17th 1781 by the officers of the 21st Regiment Virginia Militia and Volunteer Companies of Gloucester. (Montague, p. 4) The more elaborate monument was not erected until 1883. This first simple shaft remained in place into the twentieth century but was finally demolished. Gloucester did not mark its own surrender site until 1981. Courtesy of the Gloucester Historical Committee

The Bryan brothers in their later years: John Randolph Bryan II, the aeronaut of the Civil War; St. George Tucker Coalter Bryan (enlisted in 1861 at 18); Joseph Bryan (enlisted in Mosby's Rangers in 1864); and the Reverend Corbin Braxton Bryan, the youngest. Courtesy of Virginia Historical Society; photo by Foster Studio

CHAPTER FOUR
Struggle and Rehabilatation
1861–1890

On April 4, 1861, the Virginia Constitutional Convention voted two to one against secession. John Tyler Seawell, Gloucester representative, voted with the minority. Gloucester accepted the decision but when on April 12 Fort Sumter was fired on and on April 15 President Lincoln asked for troops, Virginia—forced to fight on one side or the other—seceded. Gloucester had long proved her loyalty to the Union. Now as leaders and citizens saw it, she would fight to defend her homes and her neighbors. Already there were four companies within the regiment of militia in Gloucester, and a new company was "formed to fight." Although known as the Botetourt Guards, this company was commonly called the "Gloucester Redshirts" and became an artillery company. Believing in preparedness and certainly not yet at war, Gloucester had five volunteer companies drilling in early 1861. Before the surrender in 1865, one-fifth of Gloucester's white male population of five thousand would be in the military service of the Confederacy. For the first year of the war Gloucester's men indeed defended their own homes. Fortifications at Gloucester Point were strengthened and rebuilt under the direction of engineer Charles Dimmock and manned, lightly at first, by a few men under Lt. John Thompson Brown.

On May 7, 1861, *The True Blooded Yankee*, a small armed steamer from Fortress Monroe, attempted to enter the York River. Brown opened fire with his light

---

* The author relied heavily upon Ludwell Lee Montague's book, *Gloucester County in the Civil War*, in writing this chapter.

THE FORTIFICATIONS AT GLOUCESTER POINT

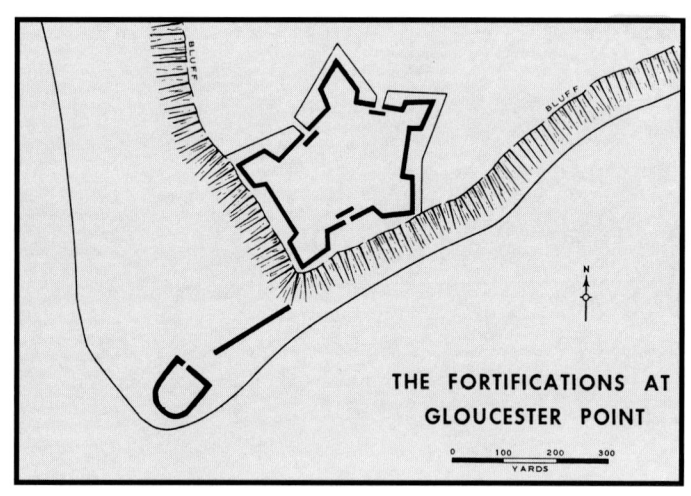

These fortifications at Gloucester Point were engineered by Charles Dimmock. The main battery on the point was protected by the large fortification three hundred yards above on the bluff. Each of the five bastions there had an emplacement for guns, many of them belonging to the two artillery companies from Richmond. King and Queen Cavalry were stationed at Ware Church and Light Dragoons established outposts in Guinea. Camp sickness prevailed among the troops crowded together at Gloucester Point. Some of the ill were taken home. Dr. Phillip Taliaferro set up a hospital at his home, Burgh Westra. The sick were sheltered and nursed at other homes also—among them Sherwood and Rosewell. From Montague's Gloucester County in the Civil War, *p. 16*

guns and the *True Blooded Yankee* promptly withdrew. These were the first shots of the war in Virginia. Realizing the vulnerability of the defense at Gloucester Point, the *Yankee* returned in two days to find a changed situation. Colonel William B. Taliaferro of Gloucester had arrived to take command. He called up the volunteer companies from Gloucester and secured ammunition and guns from Norfolk. So when the *Yankee* reappeared, she was greeted with fire that was soon realized to be superior to her own ability. The speedy withdrawal was very heartening to the Gloucester people, but perhaps encouraged them to believe that victory would be easy.

Colonel Taliaferro was soon called from Gloucester Point to Richmond and sent to western Virginia which was being invaded by troops from Ohio. At Gloucester Point, Powhatan Robertson Page, now a major, was in command and the volunteer companies had been succeeded by or converted into regular troops, mostly from Gloucester and nearby counties. A new company, to be known as the Gloucester Grays, was organized by Patrick Henry Fitzhugh; he was elected captain and sent to Richmond to buy material for uniforms; he selected gray cloth. At this time gray had not been accepted as the official color for the Confederacy but each company chose its own color. Perhaps this was another first for Gloucester.

Gloucester had yet another first when John Randolph Bryan of Eagle Point, then a lieutenant in the Thirty-second Virginia Infantry, volunteered for a surveillance mission in the balloon which General Johnston, stationed at Yorktown, had acquired. Although inexperienced as an aeronaut and with balloons, Bryan was very successful in his observations over the Peninsula. Bryan was sent on two more balloon flights. The second was also successful and the third was scheduled for a moonlight night. Bryan ascended as usual but suddenly found that the balloon was free and drifting with every rift of the wind (on land an onlooker had become entangled in the rope and to rescue him a comrade had cut it). Bryan, helpless to do more than wait for the eventual return to earth, drifted over enemy territory, over heavily wooded areas, over a wide expanse of water in which he prepared to swim and, finally, when the balloon was nearing the earth he recognized familiar grounds in Gloucester. He slid down the dangling rope, tied it to a tree and sat down on the ground exhausted. Soon Bryan returned to his earlier assignment with General Magruder and became a staff officer in the Army of Northern Virginia.

On May 1, 1862, General Joseph E. Johnston realized that his defenses at Gloucester could not stand against McClelland's superior guns and forces. It was commendable that Johnston had been able to delay McClellan so long. The

Taken from a drawing of an inner view of the Gloucester Point Fortifications of 1861. Looking out over the York River Battery 1. By an unknown artist. Courtesy of the Virginia State Library Archives

men marched in good order from Gloucester Point to Gloucester Court House where they were met with acclamation and refreshments by friends and family. Major Page stayed at the Point. Having shipped thirteen guns to Richmond the night before, he used the two remaining to delay the enemy occupation of Yorktown.

With the movement of troops from Gloucester Point the county felt abandoned and was. Although the Federals occupied the fortifications on the fourth of May and held them through the war, they made no advances into the county. They were a most unwelcome presence but they appeared not to be an immediate threat. Most of the Gloucester troops joined the Army of Northern Virginia and throughout the next two years the officers and men were widely deployed in Confederacy defense.

The first Gloucester officer to die in battle was Lt. William Jones Baytop who fell at Seven Pines when he was leading the Gloucester Redshirts. During the four years of the war Gloucester was to lose 152 men; of these, seven were officers and five held the rank of major or above; 33 Gloucester men attained officer rank.

No major battles occurred in Gloucester but her population suffered harassment and severe loss of property. When troops moved out and Gloucester Point was lost to the enemy, two—and later a third—partisan companies were formed and located on or near the western and northern borders of the county. These companies were made up of boys under eighteen and men over thirty-five or otherwise judged unfit for service in the army. They had no uniforms and supplied their own horses, ammunition and guns. Until they were absorbed into the militia near the end of the war these partisan companies served to harass the enemy, intercept communication with Richmond, and prevent depredation of local farms. Despite the vigilance of the partisans the enemy soldiers burned

William Booth Taliaferro (1822-1898), experienced in the war with Mexico, was soon promoted from colonel to brigadier general. He was placed in command at Gloucester Point but almost immediately shifted to Richmond. He served with Jackson in the Valley Campaign, in West Virginia, back and forth in the defense of Richmond and was with General Johnston in North Carolina when news reached them of Lee's surrender at Appomattox. Courtesy of the Virginia Historical Society

Eagle Point, built by John Lewis about 1760, was bought by John Randolph Bryan before the Revolution. Several years later the Bryans moved away but returned before the Civil War. They owned it for many years after most of the Bryans were living in Richmond. There is a family cemetery on the island. The Bryan family appears to have retained an affection for Eagle Point, Abingdon Church, and Gloucester County. Courtesy of the Gloucester Historical Committee

the store at Gloucester Court House, barns and mills throughout the county and, finally, the county jail. Among the homes deprived of horses, grain, cattle, sheep, swine, and poultry were White Marsh, Glen Roy, Exchange, Elmington, Dunham Massie, Rosewell, Fairfield, Marlfield, Burgh Westra, Warner Hall and doubtless others not on record. Of course many of the homes were damaged and in some cases severely plundered, although official orders forbade this. Gloucester was fortunate that most homes were not burned.

When the inevitable surrender occurred at Appomattox and was concluded on April 12, 1865, Gloucester's surviving men were widely dispersed. Grant's terms were generous for each Confederate who claimed a horse was allowed to keep it, so each member of the cavalry at Appomattox could ride home. The Gloucester infantry men would walk the 175 miles to their homes. Captain Thaddeus Fitzhugh headed for Fredericksburg and expected to join Mosby, who disbanded his men on April 21; Joseph Bryan was then free to return to Eagle Point. General Taliferro and Major Peyton Page were in North Carolina with General Johnston and they started home as soon as Johnston surrendered on April 26. Captain Thomas Jefferson Page learned of the surrenders when he reached Havana in the CSS *Stonewall*. On the eleventh of May Page sold the ship to the Spanish for just enough to pay off his crew and took passage for Italy where he rejoined his family. The last Confederate flag was taken down at Galveston on June 2. From there James New Stubbs had gone with General Magruder to Mexico.

With serious misgivings about both the value and morality of slavery, most Gloucester men fought for the protection of their homes and families—not for slavery, not even for state's rights, except in a general way. This war, in which brother sometimes fought against brother, generated more bitterness than either of the wars against the English. It caused more deaths too. Yet tales of gallantry and compassion have ameliorated the sorrow which filled the hearts of the men and women who went down in defeat. The valor and courage of the Gloucester women of the Confederacy is commemorated by a tablet on the wall of Gloucester Court House. The men who gave their lives for the cause are listed on the monument on the Court House Green. This monument stands also to honor those who lived to come home and, as General Lee instructed, "work for Virginia to build her up again, to make her great again" (this was his response when at White Marsh after Appomattox he was asked what the people of Virginia should do now).

There was a long, hard road ahead. Men who had never worked in the field followed the plow; women who had never worked in the kitchen except as instructors cooked three meals a day, and often they tended the garden and sometimes worked in the field too. Ex-slaves often worked in the house for their "keep." Those who had worked in the fields lined the fences of the big plantations every Monday morning hoping to be hired. Neighbors helped neighbors and black and white helped each other. With gardens and pigs, perhaps a cow, and the ever abundant waters Gloucester slowly made her way back, not to her former wealth, but to a sustaining economy and to a lifestyle reminiscent of the one she had enjoyed before the war. Virginia was fortunate in that she did not suffer the destruction and humiliation imposed upon some of the southern states during the period known as Reconstruction.

There were many private schools in Gloucester before the Civil War; some of these were continued after the war. Virginia adopted a public school system in 1871. The first superintendent in Gloucester was the Reverend William E. Wiatt; he was followed by William ap Walker Jones. William F. Hogg was a long time in the office. The Reverend R. A. Folkes succeeded to the office in the early years of the twentieth century; graded schools and high schools were established in the county under his tenure.

During the war Federal encampments had been made in Ware and Abingdon churchyards and horses had been stabled in Abingdon Church. Repairs had to be made and of course money was scarce. All of the churches seemed to grow stronger in these difficult times.

Major Powhatan Robertson Page (1822-1864), with forethought and courage, stayed behind when General Johnston evacuated Gloucester Point in May of 1861. The Confederate troops marched north to join those at Richmond while Page, with the few remaining, stayed at the Point and fired away at Federal infantry approaching Yorktown. In retaliation the Federal gunboat fired on Shelly, a Page home, when it finally came up the York River. Powhatan Page, then a colonel, was mortally wounded at Petersburg on June 17, 1864. Courtesy of Cecil W. Page

Captain William Jones Baytop was the first of Gloucester's men to die in battle. He was leading a charge at Seven Pines. Baytop was of the third generation of that name to lead the Gloucester Militia. Courtesy of the Sinclair Family; photo copy by Bob Bailey

Thomas Jefferson Page served in the Confederate Navy as a captain. In 1863 Page was sent to France to wait for the completion of the two ironclads building at Liverpool. When the Stonewall was completed and after some difficulty in claiming her, Captain Page was placed in command in 1864. The ship was difficult to handle in stormy seas. After a slow voyage in the C.S.S. Stonewall, Page reached Havana and heard the news of the surrender. He was able to sell the ship to Spain for enough to pay off the crew. He went to Italy to join his family there. Later the United States reimbursed Spain and the Stonewall came to the United States. *Courtesy of Cecil W. Page, Jr.*

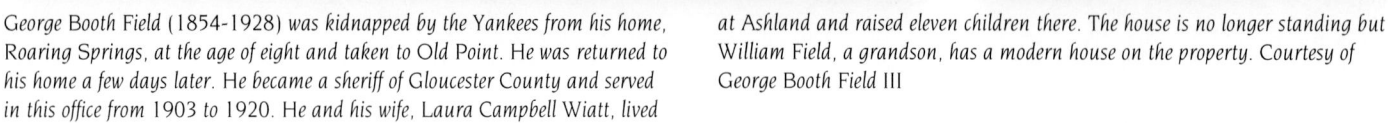

George Booth Field (1854-1928) was kidnapped by the Yankees from his home, Roaring Springs, at the age of eight and taken to Old Point. He was returned to his home a few days later. He became a sheriff of Gloucester County and served in this office from 1903 to 1920. He and his wife, Laura Campbell Wiatt, lived at Ashland and raised eleven children there. The house is no longer standing but William Field, a grandson, has a modern house on the property. *Courtesy of George Booth Field III*

Major Jefferson Sinclair and his five brothers enlisted in the Confederate Army from Hampton but they had a home in Gloucester and their families lived at Marlfield in Robins Neck throughout the war. Jefferson lived at Marlfield after he retired from service and it was the home of his descendants until the middle of the twentieth century. Courtesy of the Sinclair Family

Both Abingdon and Ware churches served as encampments for Federal and Confederate soldiers. Abingdon's interior was so badly damaged that regular services were not held there until after repairs were made in 1867. Immediately after the close of the war a service was held in the ravaged Abingdon. The congregation was moved to see that the first line of the Te Deum placed above the reredos in December 1861 in holly leaves remained. In thanksgiving that their church was standing after the conflict the first line of the Te Deum was printed in gold leaf. The words remain after several renovations and a major restoration in 1985 as a constant reminder of gratitude to God. The reredos at Abingdon is said to be the finest remaining in the colonial churches of Virginia. Courtesy of the Daily Press

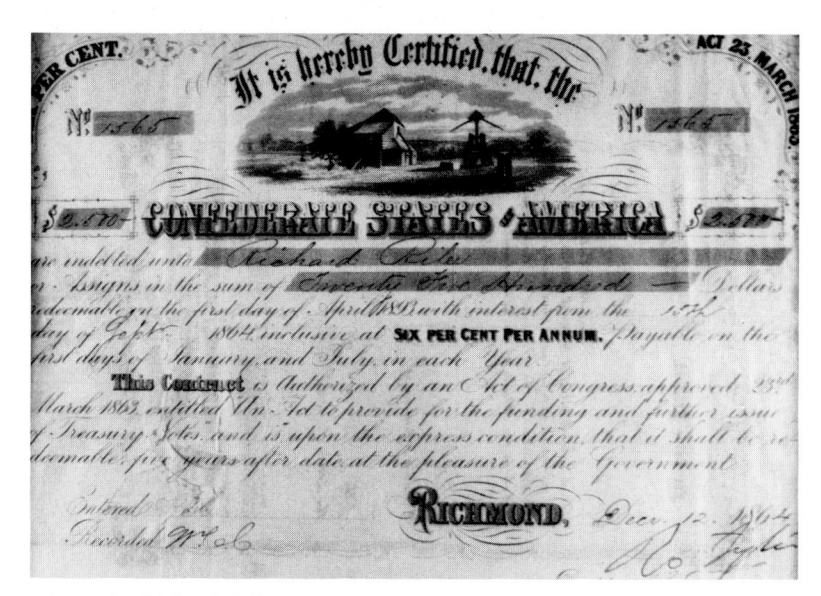

When Richard Rilee of Shelly Ford, Ark, Va., lent the Confederacy $2,500 he probably knew that his chances of collecting interest or being repaid were slim. Having been a prosperous farmer and a constable of the county he was fighting for the Confederacy and, like many others, he was willing to risk both his life and his fortune. Courtesy of Cecil C. Fary

Gloucester has regularly paid tribute to the men and, more recently, to the men and women who have served our country in time of war but only for the War Between the States has Gloucester memorialized the women at home. Courtesy of the Gloucester Historical Society

64

Parts of a Parrott Rifle

Recognized by its wrought iron jacket and its rifled barrel, the parrott rifle was used during the Civil War (1861-1865)
The family of the late Mr. Robert Stokes, who had the rifle in their possession for 70 years, presented it to Gloucester County in 1978.
Placed on this site - Dec. 1980 - by the Glou. Historical & Bicentennial Committee

The Parrot rifle at Tyndall Park and the one-hundred dollar bill issued by the Virginia Treasury in 1862 remain as mementoes of the struggle made by the Commonwealth and the South from 1861 to 1865. Courtesy of R. Edward Brown and the Sinclair Family

Exchange was built by the Buckners in the eighteenth century and exchanged with Matthew Anderson for the larger Concord, thus acquiring its name. From Anderson it was inherited by the Dabneys and remained in this family until circa 1925. It is on the North River and was originally a part of the Elmington tract. Courtesy of the Gloucester Historical Society

Students at Sherwood. Courtesy of Donald R. Perritt

After the war men began to worry about the time lost in the education of their children. New schools were started and old ones were refurbished. Several homes were opened to neighborhood children and some to boarding students; among them were Sherwood, Hickory Fork House, and Valley Front (not pictured). Mr. Tabb's Gloucester Academy at Summerville was continued into the twentieth century. Free School House on Peasley property opened its doors again and the nearby children went to school there.

Hickory Fork House. Courtesy of Gloucester Historical Committee

Gloucester Academy. Courtesy of Wyatt B. Carneal, Jr.

Old Free School. Courtesy of Wyatt B. Carneal, Jr.

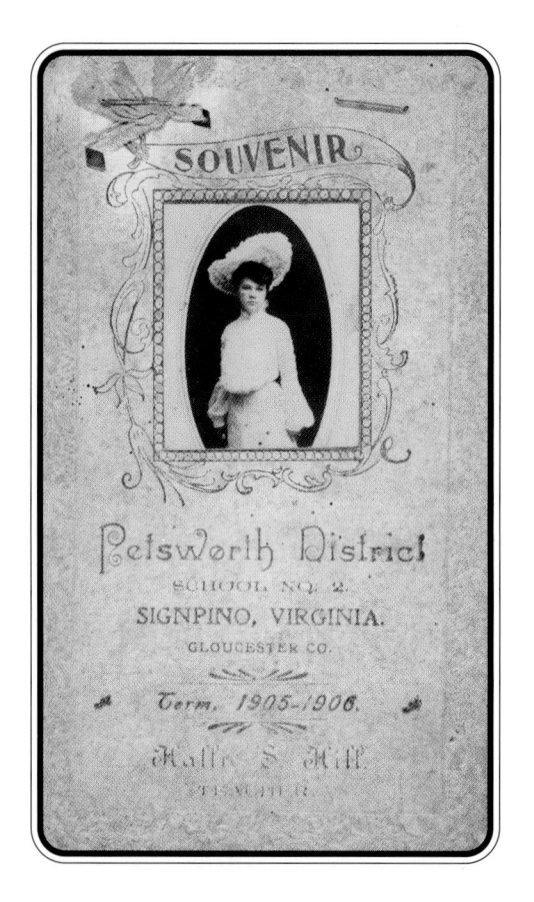

Public schools became a reality in 1871. A superintendent was appointed and soon small schools were distributed throughout the county. Among the early public schools in the county was Signpino, with a large number of Grays, Horsleys, and Wiatts attending. The souvenir card probably pictures the teacher of the 1905-06 session. The picture of the children was taken before 1910. Courtesy of Elizabeth R. Gray

Martin School was at Woods Cross Roads and was taught by the Misses Marie and Bates Lamberth. It was discontinued about 1920. Courtesy of Elizabeth R. Gray and Margaret Lamberth

Robin's Neck one-room school became Naxera Graded School with three rooms. A few of the older children are pictured here. Left to right are Edgar Emerson, Vernetta Deal (standing), Rudolf Sterling, George W. Sinclair, and Jefferson K. Sinclair (lying). Courtesy of the Sinclair Family

The first school bus in Gloucester was made and driven by Henley Roane. He drove it from Cash to Botetourt High School for nine years beginning in 1924. Henley was graduated from Randolph-Macon College and later entered the ministry. Courtesy of Elizabeth R. Gray

The first school at Achilles was across from the present school and was taught by Miss Jennie, about 1913. Courtesy of Sandra P. Hogge

69

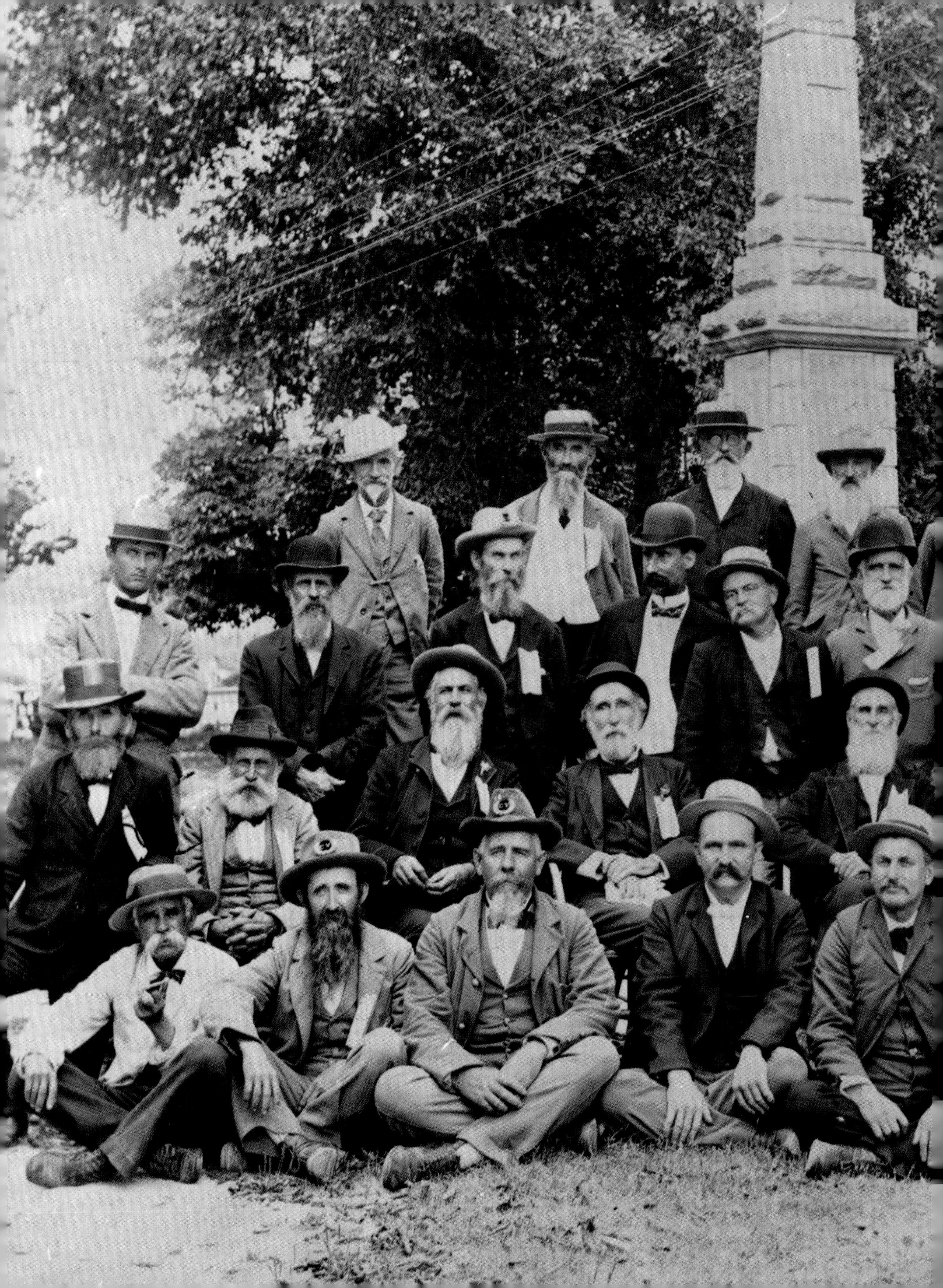

In 1889 the Confederate Monument was unveiled on the Court House Green and Gloucester's Confederate Veterans—Page-Puller Camp, C.S.A.—gathered around it. Twenty-eight years had passed since the surrender. Front Row: William Waddell, Henry Enos, Charles Catlett, William R. Thruston, Maryus Jones, J. R. Bridges, R. C. Byrd, and A. F. Fitzhugh. Second Row: J. L. Stubbs, John Brown, Joseph Hall, General William B. Taliaferro, William E. Wiatt, John B. Donovan, Thomas Moore, J. L. Philpotts, Alex Shackelford, and W. A. Smith. Third Row: William T. Williams, John Williams, A. T. Wiatt, James L. Taliaferro, S. V. Corbell, Thomas S. Taliaferro, Richard M. Page, the Reverend William Byrd Lee, George Washington Walker, W. L. Enos, and W. A. Robins. Back Row: Dr. W. F. Jones, T. P. Fary, T. J. Stubbs, Wilbur Mason, Thomas Smith, James N. Stubbs, A. M. Pointer, and W. K. Perrin. Courtesy of Alex L. Wiatt

The Pocahontas Garage supplied gas and oil, repaired cars, and held the Oakland-Pontiac agency in the 1920s. No doubt this building also housed groceries and household supplies. Courtesy of Sandra P. Hogge

CHAPTER FIVE
Recovery
1890-1917

From 1865, Gloucester County—and all of Virginia—was under Federal rule. Gloucester chose its own Board of Supervisors in 1870 and the county made great efforts to regain a lost way of life. By 1890 considerable progress had been made. The county government was stable, laws were properly enforced; public schools were distributed throughout the county; several stores were operating successfully, and four Protestant denominations were building and supporting churches in needed locations.

The people of Gloucester were ready to memorialize its past, forget its tragedies, and move into the future. The monument to the county's fallen Confederates had been erected in 1889; now the area around it once more became the center of business. Five stores began operating in the village, the jail was rebuilt on Court House Green, the Tidewater Telephone Company erected a two-story office building, the Gloucester Bank was established, and Court Day, held on the first Monday of each month, again brought the diverse interests of the county together. During the early years of the twentieth century Gloucester did not prosper, but the county did achieve a degree of economic stability.

Employment was found on the larger farms, in sawmills and in timber, in blacksmith shops, in boat building, and on the water. Many people worked their own small acreage for food and worked elsewhere for a small amount of cash. There was an exodus of young males from the county to find jobs in the cities.

Business was booming around the Court House. The telephone company built the two-story brick building. W.E. Corr owned and operated a general store in the frame building (right). The unpaved street is rather muddy. Courtesy of the Daily Press

Gloucester's Main Street: Left to right are J.H. Martin's store, Bank of Gloucester with its imposing columns, the telephone building. The paling fence around the Court House Green is evident. Cars had not yet supplanted horse-drawn vehicles. Courtesy of Elizabeth Harwood

74-2

The young blacks—men and women—also fled the county to find employment, usually to Baltimore or Philadelphia, less often to New York.

Even so, Gloucester remained a haven for these earlier inhabitants. Children spent long weeks of summer vacation with grandparents, young married women returned for the traditional month "at home," the black people who worked away usually made it back for "big meeting" time.

It is a credit to both the black and white people of Gloucester that the abolition of slavery was accomplished while maintaining a good relationship between the two races. In looking back, most Southerners would agree that all slavery was wrong; we would like to agree with Robert McColley of Kansas who wrote, "Though chattel slavery was brutal, we must accept the testimony of honest men from all over the greater community of western civilization that nowhere was it milder than in Virginia." (McColley S*lavery and Jeffersonian Virginia*, quoted by Virginius Dabney in V*irginia: The New Dominion*, p. 191). Years later Eugene P. Rhodes, a much respected sheriff of the county said, "I would rather be sheriff of Gloucester than any other place because we have the best Negroes here in the world." Mutual respect and affection have existed and both races have placed high value on family relationships.

Thomas Calhoun Walker, born into slavery, struggled to secure an education at Hampton Institute (now Hampton University) and later as a lawyer won the respect of the legal profession of Virginia. As a lifelong resident of Gloucester he was known best for his efforts to educate the black children. The Thomas C. Walker Elementary School is named for him.

Through the schools and churches and through their own hard labor the black people have helped to bring Gloucester back from a war-torn county to one of stability and the happiness of freedom and opportunity for all.

By 1912 there were two high schools in the county; most of the other schools had adopted the graded system and some of the high school graduates were going on to college. Roads were not hard-surfaced and at times were impassable. Fields were again productive but markets were distant and shipping by boat was slow. Gloucester Point, with steamers serving Baltimore and Norfolk, was the primary shipping point. There was deep water there and the wharf was large enough for wagons and teams to drive close for loading. Other rivers had smaller wharves and less depth of water. For many years during this period and later the steamer, *Mobjack*, with Captain Caffee, was well known in Mobjack Bay as she served Severn, Ware, North and East Rivers. At Claybank, on the upper York, the pier extended a long way in order to reach deep water. To help with the transportation of luggage and freight, tracks were laid from shore to wharf. A mule was provided to pull a cart along the tracks.

Ferries have been common in Tidewater since colonial days. Ferries were provided on the York at Cappahosic and at Gloucester Point, at Freeport on the Piankatank and at other crossings on Gloucester's rivers. The early ferries were rowboats which might have room for a horse, if not he swam alongside the boat. Prices were listed at Cappahosic. Passage for a man was fifteen shillings and for a man and horse two shillings six pence; in 1780 the price for a man crossing the York had been increased to seven dollars and for his horse the same. Inflation indeed!

William Henry Ash had the ferry franchise at Gloucester Point in 1865. In 1917 his son secured it and was farsighted enough to build the first large ferryboat on the York, the *Cornwallis*. Soon after 1918 an experimental strip of concrete road was built from Gloucester Point. Automobiles were becoming common in the county, industry was growing on the Peninsula and this crossing into Gloucester offered access to Richmond and northern cities. More ferries were needed and the *Cornwallis* was joined later by the *York* and the *Gloucester*.

Gloucester, having always been a haven of hospitality, began to accept paying guests in the summer. Botetourt Hotel (Tavern) offered good food and good management but the large homes, and especially those on the water, were popular and in a few years people from the cities began to rent or erect cottages to use for summer vacations. Thus Gloucester Banks, also known as "Little Richmond" was established on the lower York River.

For a rural county Gloucester has always been rather cosmopolitan in its customs, education, and social life. Good roads, schools, and an influx of city people soon stimulated change in even the most isolated sections of the county—Guinea and the other almost waterbound areas—Ware, Saddlers, and Robins necks. Telephones, electricity, and water supplies reached some areas in the county and young men and women returning from their war travels demanded these conveniences in their homes and places of business. Tractors

Court days were much as they had been before the war. Mr. Charlie Jones of Cedar Hill never missed Court Day. He considered his attendance important for his business, which was farming, and essential to his political life. He was concerned about every aspect of the county's government and progress. Courtesy of Catesby G. Jones

The jail, burned by Federal troops, was rebuilt in 1873. The small wings were later additions. After it was not used as a jail it was used as a sheriff's office, hence the star over the door. Courtesy of the Gloucester Historical Committee; photo by R. Edward Brown

Dr. and Mrs. William Carter Stubbs of Valley Front (Gloucester) and New Orleans, were Gloucester's chief historians and genealogists in the first half of the twentieth century. Mrs. Stubbs, an experienced genealogist from Alabama, worked with her husband in the publication of books on Booth, Cook, Baytop, Catlett and Stubbs families, which included much of the county's early history. The history of the county which they planned to write was not written but the papers in the Stubbs Collection in the Swem Library of William and Mary are a rich source of information. Courtesy of the Sinclair Family

became common—indeed essential—on the farms and other machinery renovated farming methods. Boats were fitted with engines, cars and trucks were essential to the rapidly changing lifestyles, and before the Great Depression arrived in 1929, Gloucester had become a modern community.

By 1917, World War I was under way in Europe. Gloucester's population was more than twelve thousand. A second bank, the First National, had been established at the Court House. Walter Reed, who was born in Gloucester County, had discovered the cause of yellow fever and the county had put up a plaque of commemoration. The Gloucester Agricultural Fair was organized in 1912. It lasted for three days. It drew patronage from all over the county and also from nearby areas; the school children were given holiday to attend and participate.

Perhaps, because of its isolation from railroads and manufacturing, Gloucester County retained many of its colonial characteristics and customs into the twentieth century. The population, largely of Anglo-Saxon heritage, was Protestant in religion and democratic in politics (especially since 1861); it tended to be conservative, but with strong beliefs in the work ethic, in education, and in independence. Having struggled through two wars for independence they cast off slavery with some reluctance but with tolerance and real concern for its victims. In *The Honeypod Tree*, Thomas Walker, the great black lawyer, tells of a firsthand struggle to make the best use of a hard-won education and the way up from slavery to success. Thomas Walker never failed to lend a hand to his people along the way and to use effectively the help extended to him by many white people.

Young men and women, both at home and abroad, would change and bring to their home county a rapid transition into the modern era.

The customs of the county portrayed in this chapter would soon seem out-of-date in the twentieth century.

When the United States entered the war in 1917, it brought many changes to Gloucester and especially to Gloucester Point.

In Robins Neck there was an early store operated by the Deals and later by A.T. Trevilian. Robert Rhodes started a second store in this area and became postmaster for Naxera. In front of his store are Robert Rhodes and his brother, Eugene, later to become sheriff, with other family members. Courtesy of Mrs. Clementine R. Bowman

Taliaferro Store at Ware Neck about 1914—there are no cars here but two horse-drawn vehicles. Courtesy of Elizabeth Harwood

77

These stores are at Maryus and Perrin, owned by Jim Ashe and Ed Brown. These two pictures, taken in the twenties, show that the motor age had arrived. Courtesy of Sandra P. Hogge

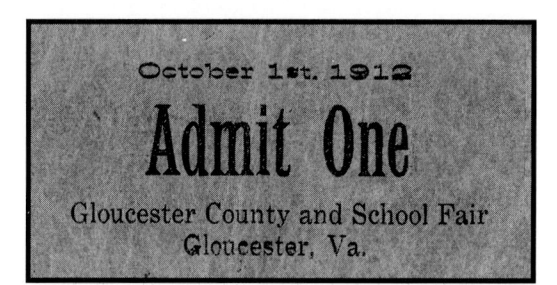

October 1st. 1912
Admit One
Gloucester County and School Fair
Gloucester, Va.

The red ribbon and ticket are from the first Gloucester Fair in 1912. The donor does not know their history except that they were passed down in her family. Courtesy of Mrs. Samuel Deal

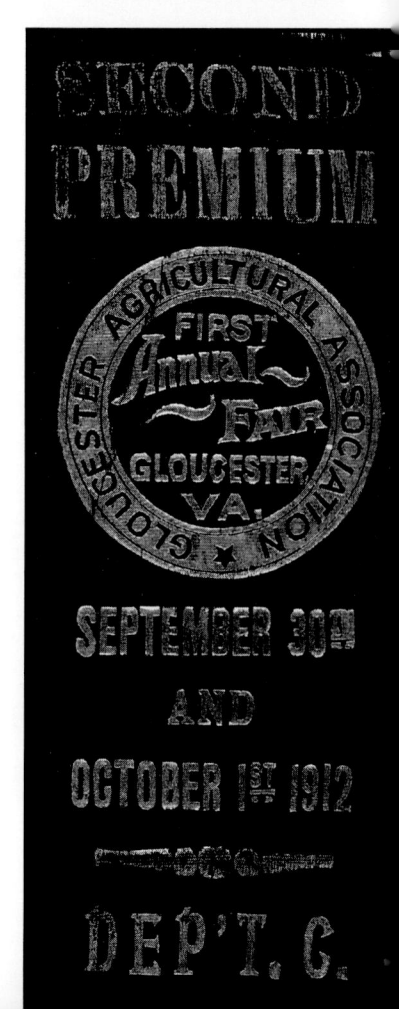

SECOND PREMIUM
GLOUCESTER AGRICULTURAL ASSOCIATION
FIRST Annual FAIR
GLOUCESTER VA.
SEPTEMBER 30TH
AND
OCTOBER 1ST 1912
DEP'T. C

Alexander Shackelford opened a shop on Court House Circle. It is now the surveyor's office of his great-grandson, Charles J. Kerns. Courtesy of Charles J. Kerns

The Fary family enlarged their timber business. This remarkable family of seven brothers, three sisters, and their mother all lived in the same house and worked in the same business. At the time of this picture only one, Marius, was married. W. T. headed the business, Ada was secretary. Standing left to right are: W. T., Marius, Emmet, Grover, Hubert, Joseph and Peter. Seated are Mrs. Marius Fary (Lillian, holding Cecil), Elizabeth, Sarah (Mother), Sallie, and Ada. Courtesy of Cecil C. Fary

Sawmills returned to business. Willie H. Dunston had a successful operation near Fox Mill Run before 1912. Courtesy of Mrs. Samuel Deal

Dock on Perrin Creek, 1920s. E.D. Brown has oil tanks on the truck and there was a boat on a railway ready for repairs and painting. A busy place! Courtesy of Sandra P. Hogge

Captain Caffee and the steamer Mobjack served the wharves in Gloucester and Mathews for many years. This was the chief means of transportation and freight to Hampton, Newport News, and Norfolk. The Mobjack also furnished joyful excursions on many summer nights. Courtesy of the Sinclair Family

81

William Henry Ashe succeeded to the York ferry franchise in 1917 and in 1921 brought the Cornwallis to cope with the increased traffic across the York River. She was the first of the modern ferries for the York crossing. Courtesy of C. David Burke

Very early the Gloucester-Yorktown Ferry offered special rates to those who crossed the river frequently. The pass shown here antedated the book of tickets which later users of the ferry service will remember. Courtesy of Mrs. Samuel Deal

GLOUCESTER-YORKTOWN FERRY, Inc.
GLOUCESTER POINT, VA.
PASS SIGNATURE CARD

Pass No._____   Date_____

No. Passengers_____

_____
Signature of Holder

Dr. Walter Reed (1851-1902), *conqueror of yellow fever, has been memorialized at his birthplace in Gloucester and nationally. He was the son of a Methodist minister, studied medicine at the University of Virginia, and served the U.S. Army in Cuba where he studied the virulent disease with great success, thus becoming a benefactor to mankind. The local hospital is named for Walter Reed and a plaque has been placed in the Colonial Court House in his honor.*
Photo left courtesy of the Daily Press, Photo below courtesy of the Gloucester Historical Committee

Gloucester's people worked hard during this period of recovery but they never forgot to play. When the ponds and rivers froze adults and children took to the ice although with limited equipment. These two pictures were taken at different places on the Ware River, perhaps in 1918, but probably earlier. At far left in the group picture is William Stephen Field. Photo left courtesy of Donald R. Perritt, Photo below courtesy of Mrs. Eleanor Field Martin

Ready for the tournament, the riders line up before the marshal issues the first call "Charge, Sir Knight!" Several Gloucester men are among the knights ready for the contest, about 1916, or earlier. Courtesy of the Sinclair Family

Roy Sinclair of Hampton is ready to accompany Miss Blanche Dimmock for a spin in her speed cart. Courtesy of Donald R. Perritt

Georgiana Sinclair (in white sweater) captains a basketball team at Farmville (now Longwood College), 1905–07. Courtesy of the Sinclair Family

Elizabeth Lewis Noland has a birthday, her fourth, at Sherwood. She is surrounded by cousins, ages one to six. Back Row: Selden Graham, Katherine Graham, and Elizabeth Noland. Front Row: Marion Rhodes, Sallie Jones, and John Tabb Fisher. Note that all are wearing white and that Tabb is dressed just like the little girls—maybe that is why Sallie is giving him such a baleful look! Courtesy of Donald R. Perritt

Knee breeches, white collars and bow ties were prescribed wear for pre-teen boys in the nineties. Courtesy of Donald R. Perritt

Aunt Jennie at Sherwood. Courtesy of Katherine Lewis Pickett

White was appropriate for young blacks and their dolls when at the "Big House." Courtesy of Donald R. Perritt

Hats were "musts" for tea in the yard. The bigger the better! Courtesy of Donald R. Perritt

And speaking of bigger—what about the shoulders of this "shirt-waist"? Courtesy of Donald R. Perritt

The Dimmock twins, Minna, on the left, and Blanche. These identical twins were known for the pranks they played and for their high spirits when they were growing up. Courtesy of Donald R. Perritt

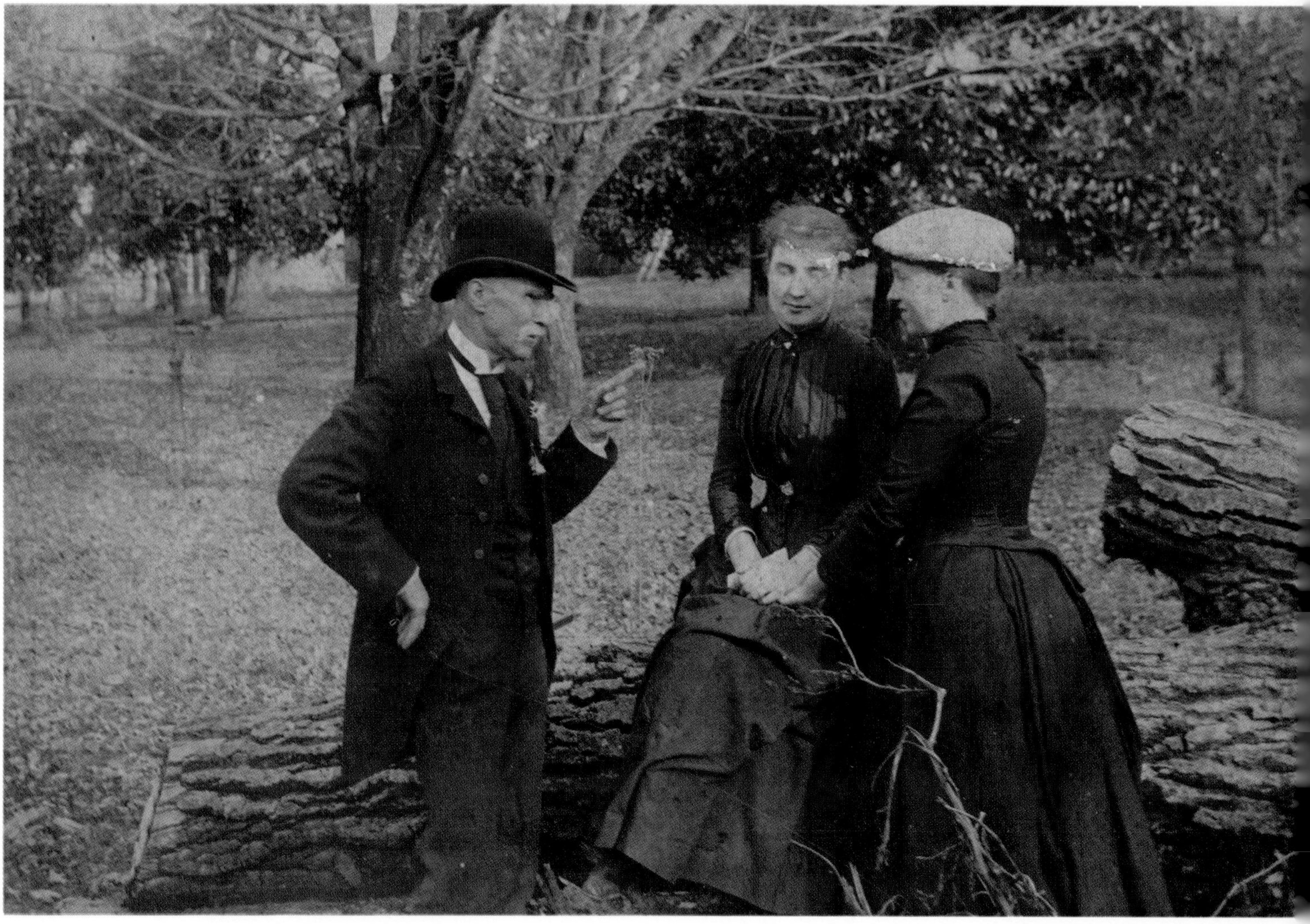

Mr. Phil Tabb, owner of White Marsh, is seen here with Miss McKee, the governess, and his daughter Cassie, at White Marsh, circa 1892. Mr. Tabb lived in New York, but he often brought his friends to Gloucester. They were hosted by Mr. and Mrs. James Sinclair who managed the house and farm. The second picture shows the size of the staff at White Marsh. Mr. Tabb is standing in the center and Mrs. and Mr. Sinclair are to his right. Courtesy of the Sinclair Family

Gloucester oystermen are proficient in the use of tongs, accustomed to the early hours, the hard work, the vagaries of wind, water and tide, and the uncertainties of motors. They know the ways of the oyster and they can bring in a "few bushels" even though the mollusks are scarce and the weather is bad. This scene is at Cappahosic. Courtesy of the Daily Press

CHAPTER SIX
The Period of Two World Wars 1917–1945

The United States remained on the periphery of World War I until 1917 but from the beginning she sent supplies to England and France. Eventually Germany became so aggressive in the destruction of shipping and ships that Congress joined a peace-loving president and declared war. In June of 1917 forty men of Gloucester met at the Court House and formed a company under Captain Harwood. Then drafts followed and additional volunteers enlisted. A total of 298 men went from the county and thirteen of them did not come back. Disease was prevalent in the camps at home and abroad and took its toll of the soldiers. Miss Cornelia Thornton, a Red Cross nurse from Gloucester, died in a camp in England.

Gloucester was much involved in the war because of her proximity to the shipping ports of Hampton Roads and munitions plants and stations in Hopewell and Penniman, but particularly because a large part of the Atlantic Fleet was stationed in the York River. The young sailors and the officers took their shore leave at Yorktown and Gloucester Point and the citizens in York and Gloucester offered as much recreation and hospitality as they could manage.

The fall of 1918 brought the successful end of World War I on November 11. It was a joyful time but the country was already in the grip of a severe flu epidemic. In Gloucester, the schools closed, public meetings and social affairs were banned. Family members struggled to nurse the ill and avoid the infection. The winter of 1918-19 gave Gloucester the coldest season on record and perhaps this helped to rout the influenza virus. The young people of the county enjoyed skating on rivers and creeks as well as on the fresh water ponds.

At Gloucester Court House a tablet was placed on the wall on April 5, 1919, by the women of Gloucester in commemoration of those who had died in World War I. Families and communities celebrated the safe return of the others.

Gloucester entered into the modern era. During the war great ships were anchored in the York River and sailors and their officers crowded the stores and streets of Gloucester Point. Gloucester's young men were away from home for months. They traveled, lived in strange surroundings, ate unfamiliar food, and many went abroad. Some suffered the privations and horrors of combat and were changed by it.

At home in Gloucester automobiles and big trucks, hard surface roads, and trips to the cities became a way of life. Patriotism was the order of the day. All the school children practiced the salute to the flag, stood at attention for the "Star-Spangled Banner," and learned the many new patriotic songs. The classrooms rang with "Over There," "Keep the Home Fires Burning," and others.

When the war ended in 1918 the returning troops were welcomed with extravagant celebrations. There was sadness too. Some men did not come back and some were crippled for life. Some had suffered experiences which would haunt them forever. But the focus of war had been away in distant lands and devastation and hardship had barely touched the homes of the men returning.

No doubt some of the veterans found it difficult to return to a life which had seemed so aloof from and barely aware of the shattering experience they had

Left photo courtesy of Mrs. Samuel Deal
Right photo courtesy of Cecil W. Page

Of Gloucester's 298 men in World War I only a few pictures are available: Knox Deal of Naxera, Richard Mann Page of Shelly, and John Mackie Sinclair (Jack), also of Naxera, who is shown with his entire company, second from the right, middle row. This company was stationed near Newport News at Camp Hill during the war. The personnel changed but Jack was kept busy tending and nurturing the horses which were regularly sent to the troops overseas.

Courtesy of the Sinclair Family

encountered. In most cases they soon settled into the familiar routine of home, family, work, and recreation. Jobs were found or had been held for them, the flu epidemic of 1918 had disappeared and life became normal and indeed prosperous again. Gloucester people, and especially those in the Langley Field Flyway, became accustomed to the frequency of airplanes overhead and occasional dirigibles in the sky. The sound of engines over the water was almost continuous as motorboats replaced the sailing work and pleasure craft, and gasoline and money seemed plentiful.

Gloucester continued into its modernization. Achilles High School was built and dedicated; mail and truck routes were established; new businesses were opened and Robert Farinholt started the Hudson and Essex automobile agency at Gloucester Court House. The Ford agency, established in 1915, continued to prosper. For the first time ice delivery was available to the homes because the ice plant had been built near Fox Mill Run; Coca-Cola set up a bottling works at the Court House.

The auditorium at the fairgrounds had become an important facility to the county. The Fair Trustees made it available for plays, musicals, and other community occasions. The auditorium burned in the late spring of 1921. For the first time Botetourt's graduating class held its commencement outside in front of the school building.

Superintendent of Schools R.A. Folkes resigned and was succeeded by J.W. Kenney, formerly a principal at Achilles. Boys' and girls' clubs existed in the twenties; Miss May Baulch was the counselor of the Camp Fire Girls. She went camping with them each summer but insisted she must have a real roof over her head—not a canvas tent! Clubs followed the Federally sponsored programs of agriculture and home economics programs in the high schools and the Future Farmers and 4-H Clubs were organized.

On August 23, 1933, a terrible storm hit the coast of Virginia. Wind and rain were severe but the tide was estimated at nine feet above normal high tide. All of Gloucester's lowlands were inundated and her rivers were raging torrents which carried all kinds of debris. When the two ferries on the York sought safety and shelter by going up the river with crews aboard, David Burke reported a player piano from the dance hall going up the river playing "Stormy Weather!" The loss of crops, buildings, wharves, animals and other properties in Gloucester and other tidal areas was devastating.

The Boy Scouts were organized in the county in 1934; the organization has gained in strength over the years and there are now many troops in the county.

In 1963 the lone troops of Girl Scouts in Gloucester and nearby counties

Memorial Plaque to the men of World War I. Courtesy of Gloucester Historical Society

joined the troops in Hampton and Newport News to form the Heritage Council. In 1981 this council joined with Greater Tidewater to form the Girl Scout Colonial Coast Council. There are now thirty-one Girl Scout troops in Gloucester and Mathews.

Schools prospered and there were many changes. In the county many of the smaller schools were closed as consolidation was recommended by the state. School bus service was started and functioned county wide. The Kenney Building was built to replace the old building at Botetourt but space was needed and the older structure remained and was used for a number of years.

For the first time since Reconstruction, Virginia voted for a Republican president in 1928; this represented the first major break in the one-party system over the years; it has now become quite usual for Virginia, and Gloucester, to support Republicans nationally and Democrats for state and local office—with notable exceptions.

Electric light lines came to Gloucester in 1928; the power was turned on September 8.

The Country Club was organized with a building and a 9-hole golf course.

For the first time diseased oysters were found in alarming quantity in Mobjack Bay and York River. Although oysters are still marketed from the area it is no longer the thriving business it was before disease became so prevalent.

Gloucester's population had not increased; it was still a rural county but industry was growing nearby. There were 1,246 farms in Gloucester but the average size was only forty-eight acres. Most of the farmers also worked on the water, on the few large farms or "across the river."

By 1939 many farms were shipping daffodils and the Daffodil Tour listed twenty-nine locations where daffodils might be viewed from main highways. Gloucester remained a center for the daffodils but gradually gave in to the competition of other areas and the difficulty of securing pickers for the harvest. Some blooms and thousands of bulbs are still sold from the county. The Daffodil Tour was started in 1938 and later became a Daffodil Festival, but this was curtailed in 1942 due to World War II.

Prohibition came and went, women began to vote and then came the market crash of 1929! People lost their jobs, farmers and watermen could not sell their produce, young people, who were working away came home for shelter and food. Gloucester fared well because so many families provided their own sustenance and owned their homes. There was little money but little real suffering. An emergency relief office was set up locally in the county. Programs were offered in food preservation, the Works Progress Administration (WPA) functioned in the county and some of the young men enrolled in the Civilian Conservation Corps (CCC). As before, in times of hardship neighbors helped each other. Out of the Great Depression and these welfare efforts grew Gloucester's first Social Service Department established July 1938, with Miss Emily Janney as superintendent. A Public Health Department followed with (later) a well-equipped building.

By 1939, Europe was building toward war because Germany, Italy, and Russia were all becoming aggressive toward the smaller countries. When France surrendered on June 22, 1940, and England fought on alone the United States became more concerned both because of her sympathies and because of the need to protect her shipping. On December 7, 1941, everything changed. When Japan attacked Pearl Harbor, the United States declared war at once and the country was mobilized, if not in fact—at least emotionally. Germany retaliated by declaring war on the United States and suddenly it was necessary to protect the country on two oceans and also assist U.S. allies overseas.

Once again Gloucester responded to the call. This time both men and women were accepted in the armed services though only men were included in the draft. The tide began to turn with Allied successes in Europe and Asia. In May 1945, Germany surrendered unconditionally. In August the United States dropped the atomic bomb and Japan surrendered on August 14, 1945. The war was over, but the joys of victory and peace were tempered by the horrors of nuclear destruction.

Although never really within her boundaries this war seemed more invasive to Gloucester County than the war of 1918. She shared the blackouts which were a constant reminder of possible air attacks; in the early years she knew that German submarines were immediately off her coast; her men and women not in the armed services worked in munitions plants and other supportive industries. As volunteers they worked with the Red Cross, Civil Defense, the USO and other agencies to welcome the troops home and send them on their way again, and to supply a great variety of support services.

Inspection of induction and discharge records of World War II supports an estimate of 820 persons enrolled from Gloucester. Fourteen of these did not survive. When the others came home they found the county relatively unchanged. It was still a rural community with lots of trees, open fields, unpaved roads, many waterways and little heavy traffic. But all of this was to change.

Severe weather! Tabb Gwyn feeding ducks on the ice in the winter in the late 1930s. The house and outbuildings of Mr. and Mrs. Sam Sterling can be seen beyond the boats moored in the creek. Courtesy of Wyatt B. Carneal, Jr.

Sheep were raised for wool and food. Rejected lambs like these at Sherwood, had to be hand fed and became the children's pets.
Courtesy of Donald R. Perritt

Horses and mules usually worked the farms but oxen were not unusual and very useful for heavy work.

Courtesy of Bernard L. Walton, Jr.

Courtesy of Merwyn Rhodes

Courtesy of Alma Powers Dudley

Courtesy of Donald R. Perritt

Hog killing was an annual event on every farm. This was on the farm of Malvin Powers at Naxera. Courtesy of Alma Powers Dudley

The common practice of shocking corn disappeared with modern methods and machinery. This was once a familiar scene. The combination of snow and shadow lends a serene beauty to the scene. Courtesy of the Daily Press

Daffodils became an important crop, particularly for the small operator in the twenties and thirties. In late years bulbs are sold in large quantities by several producers but fewer blooms are sent to market. Yards and other open areas still offer thousands of daffodils each spring. Courtesy of the Gloucester-Mathews Gazette-Journal

Sawn logs and smaller cuts were sent from Gloucester to West Point for shipping or to feed the pulp mill there. In the early days the transportation was most often by water. Courtesy of the Daily Press

From earliest times Gloucester has prospered on seafood. Now threatened by pollution and disease in the Chesapeake and Mobjack Bays and their tributaries, Virginia and Maryland are seeking and applying salutary measures. Gloucester waters still supply a living for many families and its products are still known in the best restaurants along the Atlantic coast—in Gloucester too! As always fish, crabs and oysters of the best quality are marketed from this area but, regrettably, in smaller quantities.

In the past, for commercial fishing, weirs were set with pound poles cut and put in position. Nets had to be made or repaired and hung. If the fishing was good it took several men to haul the seine. *Courtesy of the Daily Press and the Gloucester Historical Committee*

Crab pots have replaced the trot lines which were commonly used by commercial crabbers until about 1928. Courtesy of the Daily Press

Gloucester oystermen often joined others seeking seed oysters either for their own planting or to sell from the "rocks" in the James River. This is a buy boat loading from the catches of the smaller boats scattered over the James. Courtesy of the Daily Press

Marinas in Gloucester and nearby offer a haven to the many pleasure boats which are owned by water lovers in the nearby cities. These people are unable to care for their boats and keep them safe in stormy weather. This aerial view is of a marina on Sarah's Creek. If the marina can also provide boat repair it is assured of success. Boats have been built in Gloucester since prehistoric times. Gloucester men often build their own boats. This picture shows the shop of Roger Moorman. Courtesy of the Daily Press

These next four schools were the high schools of the county in the first half of the twentieth century. They housed seven grades as well as the four grades of high school. Botetourt shows the original building and the newer Kenney Building. A modern brick building has replaced the older one and Botetourt is now one of eight elementary schools in the county. Courtesy of the Daily Press

These pictures of the Botetourt faculty are from the 1916 Botetourt Annual. Included are Ethel Jones Corr (languages and seventh grade), Julia Wharton Groves (fifth and sixth grades, high school mathematics), Ruth Minor (third and fourth grades), Mary Annie Newcomb (English and history), Cora Raines (music), and E. Linwood Stubbs (first and second grades). Courtesy of Martha B. Sinclair

Hayes or Hayes Store High School, as it was first called, also became an elementary school. This picture is said to have been taken on its last day as an elementary school. It was replaced by the new Abingdon Elementary at Wicomico. Courtesy of the Daily Press

A large addition to the Achilles School enabled it to serve both elementary and high school students until Gloucester High School, located centrally, was opened in 1975 when Achilles, too, became an elementary school. Courtesy of the Daily Press

The Thomas C. Walker School was built and located centrally to serve all the black children of Gloucester County. It served this purpose until the schools were desegregated in 1968. It was used as a middle school for a few years and is now the Thomas C. Walker Elementary School. Courtesy of the Daily Press

The first centrally located school for Gloucester's black children built in 1954, was named for Thomas Calhoun Walker, the distinguished black lawyer of Gloucester. Mr. Walker's picture hangs in the school. To its left here are Dennis D. Forest, then superintendent of schools, and Wallace Fletcher of the School Board. Miss Grace Walker, educator and musician, stands on the right of her father's picture and beyond her is Heywood Johnson, principal of the school. The school was later enlarged and rededicated as the Thomas C. Walker Elementary School. This picture was also the focus of a Bicentennial ceremony honoring Mr. Walker at his former home. Courtesy of the Daily Press

Faculty of Achilles High School, circa 1925: Included are Miss Hattie Ashe (fifth and sixth grades), Miss Marie Bristow (second grade), Miss Bertha Hayes (third grade), Mrs. W. R. Hayes (fourth grade), Miss Katie Kemp (seventh grade), Miss Elizabeth Robins (assistant, high school), Miss Lesbia Rowe (first grade), Miss Edith Sterling (assistant, high school), and M. A. Waldrop (principal).

Faculty of Botetourt High School, circa 1925: Included are Mrs. E. B. Belcher (assistant, high school), J. S. Duff (principal), Miss Jane Edwards (third and fourth grades), Miss Pearl Moore (sixth grade), Miss Mary Plummer (fifth grade), Miss Kathryn Rowe (assistant, high school), Mrs. Minnie Spencer (seventh grade), and Miss Linwood Stubbs (first and second grades).

Faculty of Hayes High School, circa 1925: Included are Mrs. I. M. Anderton (assistant, high school), Mrs. William A. Buck (music), Miss Margie Clements (assistant, high school), S. F. Jones (principal), Miss Lucy Robins (third and fourth grades), Miss Bohmer Rudd (music), Miss Evelyn Stubblefield (first and second grades), and Miss Buford Waddell (fifth grade).
Faculties of Achilles, Botetourt, and Hayes (High) Schools taken from The Triangle, a joint publication. Courtesy of Mrs. Samuel Deal

May Day at Gloucester Training School (later Thomas C. Walker School). Mildred Cook was crowned Queen, 1954. Courtesy of the Daily Press

County-wide school celebration. Fifteen hundred students and teachers from nine schools marched together, 1934. Courtesy of the Gloucester-Mathews Gazette-Journal

The Reverend R.A. Folkes was the superintendent of schools in Gloucester from 1905 until 1921. High schools and graded schools were established during this period. Mr. Folkes was also a minister of the Baptist church and the surveyor of the county. A meticulous worker, he made the carefully designed map which lines the cover of this book. Courtesy of Catesby G. Jones

Mary Wiatt Gray (Mrs. Russell) taught for more than thirty years in the public schools of Gloucester. She also gave us, in 1936, Gloucester County (Virginia), *a history written for the school children. It is out-of-print now but contains more facts about Gloucester County than anything else that has been written. It has been invaluable to this author as it will be to the person who will someday write the complete history of the county. Courtesy of Elizabeth R. Gray*

There were several youth and club activities in Gloucester in the twenties and thirties. Some of these were sponsored by the schools. The Camp Fire Girls were organized at Botetourt High School about 1917. Miss May Baulch was the guardian. Some of the girls are shown here in official uniforms and also ready to swim at one of their annual summer camps. Their camps were held at a borrowed or rented home on the water. Miss May was an enthusiastic camper but no tents for her — she had to have a real roof over her head! Courtesy of Roberta Brown King

Camp Chespeake on the Ware River. This camp for boys was owned and directed by Dr. J. Blair Spencer. It offered a great variety of activities and attracted campers from Gloucester and elsewhere. The camp burned in the thirties and was not restored. Courtesy of Cecil W. Page

Boy Scout Troop 122 of Gloucester Point, readying the camp at the Walton Farm, Adner. Left to right are Mr. Henry Midgett, Dennis Walton, and B.L. Walton, Sr. Note the neatly cut and stacked wood and other preparations. Courtesy of Mrs. B.L. Walton, Sr.

This Boy Scout stands on the bank of the York River near Camp Okie as he gives the evening bugle call. Courtesy of the Daily Press

The Boy Scouts built this log cabin on school property at Botetourt in the late twenties. It has been used for many purposes. Scouts still use it on occasions. Courtesy of the Gloucester Historical Society. Photo by Lane's Studio

Boy Scouts help the Community during World War II. Courtesy of the Gloucester-Mathews Gazette-Journal

Mumfort View 4-H Club. This group at Hayes successfully petitioned the state in 1982 for street signs in the community. Courtesy of the Gloucester-Mathews Gazette-Journal

Girl Scouts swimming at Burke's Pond, International Week, 1989. The extensive property at Burke's Pond was given to the Girl Scouts in 1972 by Mr. Fred J. Mason. It is now a well-equipped regional camp site. Courtesy of the Gloucester-Mathews Gazette-Journal

Horses and hounds have always been a part of Gloucester's life. Catesby Field, whose young colt won the silver cup, at halter. Courtesy of Eleanor Field Martin

Panoramic picture 1927. The Tidewater Fox Hunt Association was organized in Gloucester in 1926. Here are the Association members in Gloucester in 1927 ready for the Bench Show, Field Trials, Horse Show, and Hunt Ball. *Courtesy of the Sinclair Family*

Field Trials, Tidewater Fox Hunt, 1927. These pictures show the field taken in motion and Jeff B. Sinclair, on his hunter Phyllis, competing in the show which followed the hunt. *Courtesy of the Richmond Times-Dispatch*

Jousting tournaments were popular in Gloucester through the twenties and early thirties. This picture of Jack M. Sinclair was taken with his mount at full speed, circa 1920. Courtesy of the Sinclair Family

Vernon Kerns one, two, and three, participated in a costumed class at a horse show at the Botetourt School in 1937. Left to right William Vernon Kerns, son, on Cubby; Marius Vernon Kerns, father, on Bootlegger; and William Vernon Kerns, grandson, on Pocahontas. Courtesy of Charles J. Kerns.

The Great Storm of August 23, 1933, left devastation in Gloucester. Few pictures survive and probably few were taken. People were too busy rescuing people and animals and trying to save property. The necks of land between Gloucester's five rivers were completely inundated and most of the piers and wharves were swept away. The ferry Cornwallis is shown after the storm resting against the pilings of the Gloucester Point wharf until the ferry dock was rebuilt. Courtesy of C. David Burke

Wind and water wrought damage at Cow Creek Mill but the old mill weathered the storm. Courtesy of Mrs. Melvin R. Hogge

Miss Eleanor Perrin played a unique musical instrument at Goshen. Twenty-four glasses three to five inches in diameter fill the chest. When rubbed with wet fingers, the rims produce musical tones. Glasspiel and hydrodaktylopsychicharmonica are two of many names for this antique instrument. At that time, in 1956, Goshen had been in the Perrin family for 132 years. Photo by Howell Walker, copyright April 1956 by National Geographic Society

Page Rock Light, near the mouth of York River still guides the seafarer on his way. The light is electrical and automated now. Note that the bell still hangs outside and that there are curtains at the windows in this picture. Courtesy of the Daily Press

Officer raids still at Glenns, 1954. Prohibition days are past but the illegality of this still is a serious matter. Courtesy of the Daily Press

An aerial view of Gloucester Court House, about 1960. Note the large wooded and agricultural areas. These have now been depleted by houses, roads, and industrial developments. Courtesy of the Daily Press

A *dock for three ferries was added at Gloucester Point and the* York *and* Gloucester *were added to the ferry service. Courtesy of the Daily Press*

123

Powatan's chimney, built of native marl near the York River, is said to have been built at the order of Captain John Smith for the Indian chieftain, Powhatan. Its authenticity has been disputed by historians, but no one has offered any other explanation for this unique historic landmark. The chimney was badly damaged by a storm in 1888. Concern about its fate sparked the organization of the APVA but it was over forty years before the organization was able to rebuild it. Although the APVA cared for this historic structure for many years the Association never had a clear title to the property. Consequently there was great concern when the surrounding area was sold, obviously for development. The purchaser, Walter Carmine, formerly of Gloucester County, developed the property into an attractive community but graciously donated the chimney and a small area around it to Gloucester County. The APVA, because of its long concern for the structure, has agreed to maintain it. Powhatan's Chimney is easily visible from Rt. 1316. Courtesy of the Gloucester Historical Committee; photo by Bob Bailey

Everett Powers entered the service in May of 1944 at the age of twenty-three. That same year he went to France, was in the Battle of the Bulge and was wounded. Everett died in a hospital on Christmas Day. He was buried in Luxembourg but in 1948 his parents had his body brought home and interred in the family lot at Ebenezer Baptist Church in Gloucester. Courtesy of Alma Powers Dudley

Catesby G. Jones, whose joyful return from World II was shared by his family. With him here are his mother, Rosa Folkes Jones, and Sarah Bluefort, who served the Jones family for many years and was much beloved. Courtesy of Catesby G. Jones

125

Dogs and children gather to enjoy the snow on Lewis Avenue. Courtesy of the Daily Press

CHAPTER SEVEN
Changing Times
1946-1990

Nationally the long years from World War II to 1991 were characterized by "the cold war" with Russia, the Vietnam and Korean conflicts, the Watergate scandal, Congressional struggle for power, and visions of world peace in 1989 and 1990, to be followed sadly and all too quickly in January 1991 by declared war in the Persian Gulf.

In Gloucester the years from 1945 to the present were not turbulent but they brought many changes. Among the first of the school systems in Virginia to be cited for discriminatory action nevertheless Gloucester County accomplished desegregation of its schools quietly and efficiently in 1968 and an expanding school system has resulted; now there are also two institutions for higher education in the county.

The Coleman Bridge, which spanned the York River in 1952, brought a larger population to Gloucester and even before the toll was removed in 1976, it also gave easier and quicker access to the job markets on the Peninsula. Population in the county increased rapidly. Two districts, York and Gloucester Point, were added in 1971 to the three existing since 1790 and the Board of Supervisors was increased from three to five. More services were demanded and more taxes were collected. It was deemed necessary in 1970 to engage a county administrator. Since that time many other positions have been added to the county staff. In the 1990 census the county population was found to be 30,131 (later estimated at more than 33,000), one of the fastest growing areas in the country. For needed

The Coleman Bridge was opened May 8, 1952. Governor John S. Battle is pictured cutting the ribbon. Two easily identified persons are standing behind him—Bishop Henry St. George Tucker (left) and the Commandant of the Fifth Naval District (right). The bridge opened up a new era in the development of Gloucester County, accelerated when the toll was taken off in 1976, some years after the toll had paid for the bridge. Unfortunately, the Coleman Bridge has now become an obstructive bottleneck. When it is open cars may be lined up for miles on both sides. When closed it cannot accommodate rush-hour traffic. There are varying opinions as to the best solution. Meanwhile, people on both sides of the York suffer long delays. Courtesy of the Daily Press

space the county bought and restored the pre-revolution Botetourt Tavern in 1965. A new Courts and Office Building was completed in 1982.

A centrally located high school to house all of Gloucester's high school students was completed in 1975; additions to it are already needed. Gloucester now has five elementary schools, two middle schools and one high school.

Walter Reed Memorial Hospital opened near the Court House in 1977. It is now called Riverside Walter Reed Hospital because of its affiliation with Riverside Hospital in Newport News. It is the center of a large medical complex serving several counties and including Walter Reed Convalescent Center, two office buildings for medical personnel, and a Wellness and Fitness Center. There are other medical facilities near Gloucester Court House and Gloucester Point. The Francis N. Sander's Nursing Home, a gift, was opened in 1961. It has been enlarged and now adjoins Sander's Commons, an affiliated retirement home built in 1985.

After prolonged investigation the first radial well in Virginia was established at Ordinary in 1981 to serve the Gloucester Point area. A more ambitious project, the Beaver Dam Reservoir, began operating in July of 1990. This supplies water to the Court House area and south along Route 17, including the White Marsh, Ordinary, and Hayes communities with probable additions to come. This project also gives Gloucester another park which is to be opened officially in 1991. The county owned park at Gloucester Point is in heavy use and Abingdon Park near Abingdon School has been developed for the community. Ark Park (Fairgrounds) is now open for further development and use. The Parks and Recreation Department functions year-round with programs and facilities for all ages. The county now lists twenty-six recreation areas, including eight schools, twelve public landings, three parks, one beach, one rental soccer field, and one nature trail.

Temperate weather is one of Virginia's attractions and in Gloucester the cold of winter is modified by its large bodies of water and the heat of summer by plentiful shade and breezes from the sea, but there are storms of a varying nature. The tidal wave of 1933 has not been exceeded but there was a very high tide on Ash Wednesday of 1962; Hazel, an extremely severe wind storm occurred in 1952; in 1979 and 1989 storms caused considerable damage in the county. Gloucester residents, particularly those who live on the water, have learned to keep a wary eye on the weather, especially during the fall hurricane season. Although severe snowstorms are rare, "snow days" are allowed each year for the schools. Whenever snow does occur it becomes a playtime for children and sometimes for adults too. Ice skating is not as popular as in earlier times but even the salt water offers safe skating in occasional severe freezes.

Hunting has been a way of life in Gloucester since colonial days and persists today in the county. Large open fields and wooded areas offer deer, wild turkeys and game birds. Coon, possum, foxes, rabbits and squirrels frequent the woods and fields. There are several hunt clubs in the county. The James River Hunt Club, based in Hampton, has bought property in the county and schedules most of its fox hunts here. The Gloucester Hunt Club organized fox hunts and horse shows in the county until 1941. The Tidewater Fox Hunting Association was organized in Gloucester in 1926. Over the years most of its field trials have been held in the county. Many trophies and ribbons have been won by hounds of Gloucester owners.

Horses have always been important in Gloucester but in recent years outsiders have moved to the county in order to have space and facilities for their horses. Several riding schools have been developed here. The Gloucester Horse and Pony Club was organized circa 1950. Besides its annual show the club offers many other activities. The 4-H Club also sponsors a riding program with emphasis on the care and training of the mounts.

Over the years a number of annual events and/or festivals have been held in Gloucester. The Ruritan Club schedules two Seafood Festivals each year, one in May and another in October, both held at Bena.

The Christmas Parade in early December is becoming more festive each year as decorations are added, shops at the Court House stay open and features are displayed. Each year the parade grows larger and more lights blaze forth as night falls.

Under the auspices of the Gloucester Garden Club and as a part of Garden Week in Virginia, a Gloucester-Mathews Tour has been held annually in April since 1920. The Gloucester Garden Club also holds a daffodil show every year. This show is generally believed to be one of the best in the country. The Daffodil Festival, started in 1939, was discontinued in World War II. It was replaced by a pageant sponsored by the Lions Club, 1958-1965. In 1987 a Daffodil Festival Committee was formed and the Daffodil Festival is now an annual

An aerial view of the Virginia Institute of Marine Science, the county-owned beach and piers near it, and the Coleman Bridge. Since this picture was made a handsome new building has been added and the beach area has been developed into a county park. VIMS is a Division of the College of William and Mary. Located at Gloucester Point in the 1930s it was first known as the Virginia Fisheries Laboratory. It has established an international reputation for research. Courtesy of the Daily Press

affair. Eight to ten thousand people are expected to attend in 1991.

The Dragon Run Festival, held annually at Rappahannock Community College, emphasizes local history and native crafts and through publicity and a 'float' on the Dragon, it focuses attention on the exotic beauty and environmental significance of the Dragon Run.

The Greater Guinea Jubilee is a recent addition to these annual festivals. It was started in 1979 and has become more popular each year. It is held at Hayes Plaza on Route 17. This festival is built around the traditions and uniqueness of the neck of land between the York and Severn rivers which has been known as Guinea since beyond the knowledge of anyone living.

Many other events are held annually in Gloucester by the schools, churches, the various clubs,and other organizations.

Gloucester, one of the oldest of the Virginia counties, has always been aware and proud of its history but only in recent years has it made a sustained effort to record and preserve it. The Gloucester Historical Committee was appointed by the Board of Supervisors in 1969 (later to have "and Bicentennial" added to its title). It was particularly active in 1976, in 1981 and in 1987 when the Bicentennials of the Declaration of Independence, the surrenders at Yorktown and Gloucester Point and the adoption of the Constitution of the United States were celebrated. This Historical Committee has rendered an important service to the county since it was first appointed.

The county organized its first historical society in 1934 but it did not survive the exigencies of World War II. It was started again primarily through the efforts of Cary Franklin (Mrs. Warren) who in 1976-78 was chairman of the Gloucester Historical and Bicentennial Committee. The Gloucester Historical Society is organized with a number of divisions which represent and focus on the diversity of its members interests. Notable among the divisions is the Rosewell Foundation. Miss Nellie and Lieutenant Colonel Fielding L. Greaves, third generation owners of the Rosewell property, gave the ruins of the mansion and 8.746 acres of land to the Gloucester Historical Society in December 1979. Since that time the Society has made a valiant and successful effort to preserve and protect the property.

In 1990 the Board of Supervisors granted the request of Judge John DeHardit, representing several organizations of the county and many citizens, for the use of the Roane Building on the Court House Green as a county museum. It remains under the control of the Gloucester Historical Committee but will have its own Board of Directors. It will have its formal opening in 1991.

During the Bicentennial years Gloucester County received two grants, under the auspices of the Historical and Bicentennial Committee, which allowed it to conduct an archeaological survey and an intensive architectural study of the county buildings. A comprehensive report has not been published but to a limited extent the work has been continued at Gloucester Point, Rosewell, Shelly and, privately, elsewhere. The second grant received by the county resulted in research by two qualified historians and publication by the Virginia State Library of A *Guide to Gloucester County* and *Virginia Historical Manuscripts.* Dr. Louis Manarin, archivist, State Library, said this was one of the most important pieces of work to come out of the Bicentennial years.

The Virginia Institute of Marine Science at Gloucester Point, originally known as the Virginia Fisheries Laboratory, is now a division of the College of William and Mary. It has been recognized internationally for marine research. It has rendered significant service to Virginia and especially to those counties, including Gloucester, so heavily dependent on the seafood industry.

At the northern end of the county near the Middlesex line Rappahannock Community College opened its doors in 1971. It has offered opportunities to those who are college bound and to those who seek job preparation at other levels; it also serves local business and professional men by helping to provide for their special needs. Both VIMS and Rappahannock have brought well-educated and energetic people into the county with new ideas and a variety of experiences.

For many years Gloucester residents shopped in Richmond or on the Peninsula, but now almost all of their needs can be supplied locally. Most of the the older stores are gone but shopping centers, service stations and convenience stores are dotted along Route 17. Seafood, timber, and farming are still the foundation of the county's economy but supplementary businesses are well established and a wealth of new enterprises are opening weekly. Until recently there was a dearth of good restaurants in the county; now one can find good food and pleasant surroundings in several neighborhoods.

Though one bank served the county for many years there are now three with statewide connections and one owned and operated locally. The stability of these indicate a conservative but prospering economy.

In the last few decades the growth and stability of Gloucester County is also evident in its religious life. There are now at least forty-seven churches in the county, representing about ten denominations. The first Catholic church was established in 1939; it serves Gloucester, Mathews, and Middlesex counties. Among the older churches almost all have enlarged their facilities or added new buildings. Some have restored or replaced the old buildings.

These factors of growth are indicative of changing times in Gloucester and people change with the times, but there remains in this county a flavor and an appreciation of the good life which survived more than three hundred years and will, no doubt, reach into the future.

Gloucester High School, built in 1975 on Short Lane, was the first building to house all of Gloucester's high school students. It is centrally located and provides facilities for programs not previously offered. The grounds have not yet been fully developed. The students still use outdoor space at Page Middle School on Route 17 for some activities. The High School now offers tenth to twelfth grades and has almost reached capacity enrollment. Courtesy of the Gloucester-Mathews Gazette-Journal

The last year presented in this record is that of 1990. The events which brought the promise of world peace overshadowed all other happenings of the year but Gloucester continued to grow—in population, in needs, and in services. Traffic increased, new businesses opened, shopping malls were built and developed along Route 17. The schools, now eight in number, were crowded and needed additional classrooms; enlarged medical facilities were making Gloucester a medical center for a large rural area.

When the county completed the Beaver Dam project and was able to supply water to a larger proportion of its residents it was also exploring and beginning to serve other crucial needs. Mosquito control was started in certain districts in 1989. Recreation facilities have been greatly improved in the last decade. Another school is in the planning stage. Problems relative to water, sewage, waste disposal and regional cooperation are under study and plans are being made. These are indeed changing times for Gloucester County!

Gloucester basketball team goes to State two years, 1989 and 1990. Aaron Burrell shooting.

Gymnastics at G.H.S.

Gloucester High School students now compete in many activities with students from other counties and cities—in music, art, television programs, debating, essay contests, athletics, and others. They also participate with these students on many occasions. Pictured here are samples of students and teams successful in athletics. Courtesy of the Gloucester-Mathews Gazette-Journal

Field hockey, 1983. G.H.S. has many winning teams in hockey.

High jump in track-and-field meet. Donnie Rhea of Gloucester is successful.

Riverside Walter Reed Hospital is the core of a growing medical complex which now includes two professional buildings, a nursing home, and a wellness center. Through its affiliation with Riverside of Newport News the hospital is able to offer a wide variety of medical and surgical specialties. Courtesy of the Daily Press

Members of the Board of Francis S. Sanders' Nursing Home received a donation from the donor and founder for whom it is named. Mr. Sanders is seated. Standing, left to right, are Dr. Raymond Brown, Edgar Pointer, Dr. L.V. Morgan, Dr. Stanley Gray, and Wesley Morck. The nursing home was extended with a retirement complex, called Sanders Commons, in 1985. Courtesy of the Daily Press

The Beaver Dam Project started supplying water to some areas of Gloucester in 1990. Service will be extended and the park will be opened in 1991. It is intended that water will be carried to an expanding area in later years. Courtesy of the Gloucester-Mathews Gazette-Journal

A growing population demands more and better facilities for recreation. The Gloucester Parks and Recreation Department is making use of the schools and of the county's long-owned public landings. Public parks, unknown in the county until recently, are being developed. Gloucester's natural resources are also being protected and utilized. This map shows the locations of the twenty-six areas now in use and/or cared for by the Department. Courtesy of the Parks and Recreation Department

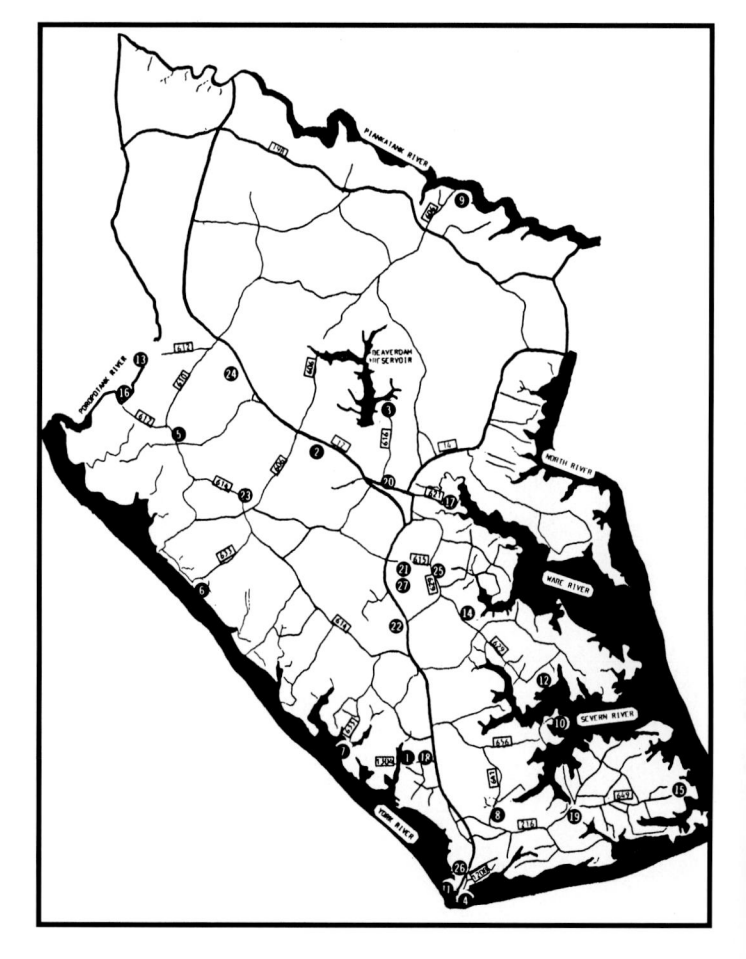

134

Hazel of the high winds hits Gloucester Court House, 1954. This was one of the most devastating storms to be experienced in the area. Fortunately the tides were not excessive. Courtesy of the Daily Press

Another severe storm topples Haynes Mill. Although not grinding at the time, this was the last mill in the county to grind corn. Haynes Mill Pond is one of the beauty spots of the county. Courtesy of the Gloucester-Mathews Gazette-Journal

Ready to go! On an autumn day when the dogs are eager—Joan LeGrand and Billy Gray, 1936. Courtesy of Elizabeth R. Gray

A 16 pound turkey bagged near Cappahosic in 1988 is held by Danny Snyder and Todd Bohannon. Which one shot it? Courtesy of the Gloucester-Mathews Gazette-Journal

Ronnie and Michael Greene checked in this nine-point deer which they shot near Ark in December 1989. It weighed 175 pounds. Courtesy of the Gloucester-Mathews Gazette-Journal

In 1966 the General Assembly named the fox hound as the official state dog. Courtesy of the Daily Press

137

Blessing of the Hounds at Eagle Point, 1968. This ceremony, a traditional practice in England, has been held in Gloucester County since the thirties by the James River Hunt Club. In the foreground, standing left to right are the Reverend Howard Mueller, rector of Abingdon Church; S.P. Stafford, Master of Fox Hounds; Powell Catlett and Jeff B. Sinclair, huntsmen; Alexander Wiatt and Severn Wallace, whips. The chosen hounds are standing by. On this occasion some of the Deep Run Hunt were guests. Courtesy of S.P. Stafford

S. Phillip Stafford, Jr., age 4 1/2, watches the ceremony. Courtesy of S.P. Stafford

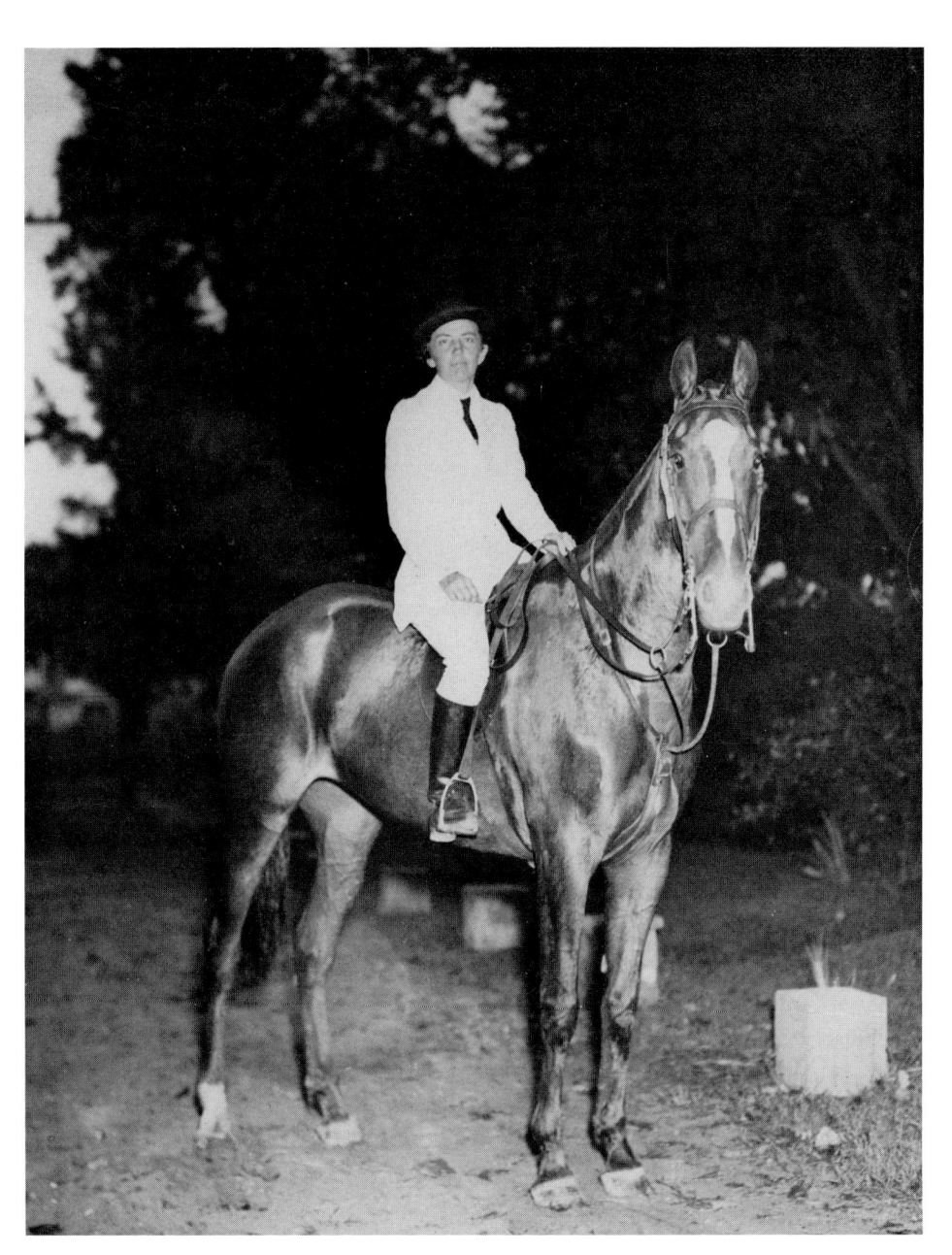

Mermaid, Indie Sinclair up, was named because as a young filly she survived the '33 storm by being taken into the house. The tide was too deep for her in the yard and pasture. Taken with flashlight, this picture is of horse and rider on the way home, having won the championship of the Gloucester Horse Show. Owner: Jeff B. Sinclair, circa 1938. Courtesy of the Sinclair Family

Two Gloucester Churches dating from colonial days are Ware and Abingdon. Ware celebrated its tercentennial in 1990 and has maintained services throughout this long period. Abingdon's early communion silver, pictured here, was given by the Burwell family. One piece is inscribed 1702. The flagon and a large paten were damaged in the Rosewell fire (1916) and have been restored. This silver has been twice exhibited at the Virginia Museum. Courtesy of the Daily Press; photos by Bob Bailey

White Hall, with its spacious grounds and garden, was open for Garden Week. This handsome home is believed to incorporate a smaller structure built by Francis Willis soon after 1666. It was the home of Willis, Corbin, and Byrd families well into the twentieth century. Courtesy of the Gloucester-Mathews Gazette-Journal

Each year, prior to the Dragon Run Festival, Rappahannock Community College sponsors the Dragon Run Float. A limited number of people traverse the Run by canoe. The mystic beauty of the trip is due to the exotic vegetation and the cypress growth found on the banks and in the water. The festival, which features local crafts, customs and history, brings several thousand people to the college campus each year. Courtesy of the Gloucester-Mathews Gazette-Journal

Rappahannock Community College has two campuses — one in Northern Neck near Warsaw, the other in upper Gloucester County. The entrance to the Gloucester campus is pictured with students entering on a warm day. Courtesy of the Daily Press

Many shops are open and various contests are held at the time of the Christmas Parade. Sinclair Rhodes, a former sheriff of the county acted as Marshal in 1984. His wife, Merwyn, formerly an art teacher in Gloucester public schools, is with him. The lighted trees along Main Street blaze with sparkling color as soon as darkness falls. Courtesy of Merwyn Rhodes

Courtesy of the Gloucester Historical Committee

May Day was celebrated at Botetourt High School for a number of years. At Botetourt, Christine Hogge was crowned Queen of the May in 1955. Her young attendants smile in the limelight. The May Day included a number of costumed dances by the younger children, as this circa 1947 group. Courtesy of Mrs. Melvin R. Hogge

143

The Rudducks raised prize-winning Black Angus when they lived at White Hall. Courtesy of the Daily Press

Mrs. William Gray is ambitious; having won locally she is selecting canned food to enter in the 1958 State Fair in Richmond. She is mirrored in a walnut sideboard which was originally in the Selden Family. Courtesy of Elizabeth R. Gray

A costume ball at the Gloucester Country Club about 1955. In the center is Van Bibber Sanders, a well-remembered bachelor and social leader in the county. Courtesy of Catesby G. Jones

Golfers on the course near the Club House at Gloucester circa 1950. Courtesy of the Daily Press

Concerts are held on the Court House Green several times each summer. Courtesy of the Gloucester-Mathews Gazette-Journal

Tonging for Oysters. This was one of many competitions held at the Greater Guinea Jubilee in 1988. The Jubilee has been held annually since 1979. The Jubilee is held at Hayes Plaza on Route 17. Since water is not available oysters are tonged from a platform. The festival focuses on the customs and talents of the people of Guinea, a community between the Severn and York rivers. The origin of the name has been debated but never established. Courtesy of the Gloucester-Mathews Gazette-Journal

Olen Lewis was writer, director and performer in the annual Lions Club Show. It was sadly missed when discontinued in 1988. Courtesy of the Gloucester-Mathews Gazette-Journal.

A Kentucky native, Jim Owsley has been making music and musical instruments in Gloucester for thirty years. He has made fifty-eight mandolins and also banjos, violins, and dobros. He has held musical sessions at his home regularly since 1963 and has attained fame here for his country music and also abroad through Southern Country Magazine *of Southampton, England. Courtesy of the Gloucester-Mathews Gazette-Journal.*

Margaret Lamberth, chairman of the Gloucester Historical Committee, reports to the Board of Supervisors for 1990. Appointed for the first time in 1969, the Committee has charted the county's activities through the Bicentennial years, nurtured the organization of the Gloucester Historical Society, is responsible for the Roane Building which has been designated to house the Gloucester Historical Museum, and continues to contribute in immeasurable ways to the preservation and promotion of the county's history. *Courtesy of the Gloucester-Mathews Gazette-Journal*

Pre-historic bones: James Morgan, always an environmentalist as well as a pharmacist, found the long-buried bones of a plankton-eating whale in Fox Mill Run. This seems to reveal an interesting phase in the geology of our county since the scientists have estimated this whale lived five to seven million years ago. Courtesy of the Gloucester-Mathews Gazette-Journal

The Gloucester County seal was found by Robert Robins, formerly of Ware Neck. It was confirmed by the Board of Supervisors in 1974 as the official seal of the county. It was incorporated in brass and iron trivets to commemorate the Bicentennial of 1976. The beehive stands for loyalty, unity, and industry. Courtesy of the Gloucester-Mathews Gazette-Journal

One of the many entries in the Bicentennial Parade on Main Street, Gloucester, August 1976.

Rosewell ruins and grounds are open at stated times during the year and on request. The first picture shows how steel bars have been used to stabilize the walls and massive chimneys. More recently the chimneys have been repaired and recapped. Courtesy of the Gloucester Historical Society

Courtesy of B. L. Walton, Jr.

Bicentennial Headquarters, 1976, on the John Hudgins property, Route 17. Note the United States and Bicentennial Flags spreading in the breeze. Courtesy of the Sinclair Family

Supervisor Everett Rich prepares for burial of significant mementoes and messages from Gloucester and its Bicentennial celebration of 1976; these are to be taken up in another one hundred years when the Tricentennial is celebrated. Courtesy of the Gloucester-Mathews Gazette-Journal

A market place demonstration by the Triangle Squares, a part of the 1976 celebration of the Bicentennial. Courtesy of Merwyn Rhodes

Countrie So Faire. This is the title of the 1976 pageant featuring Gloucester's history. It had a cast of five hundred local people and a number of local horses! It was given for three successive evenings on the grounds of the Gloucester Intermediate School (now Page Middle School) and sponsored by the Gloucester Historical and Bicentennial Committee and a corporation formed for this purpose. The writer and director of Countrie So Faire was Michael Whaley of the Rogers Company, New York. Courtesy of the Gloucester-Mathews Gazette-Journal

This picture, taken October 1981, shows the chairman of the Board of Supervisors, W.E. Belvin, and the vice-chairman, Bruce Long, presenting the monument which marks, for the first time, the site of the British surrender in Gloucester to the French and American Forces. The inscription says: Near this place on October 19, 1781, a surrender occurred one hour after the surrender at Yorktown. The British troops under Lieutenant Colonel Banastre Tarleton surrendered to the French Brigadier General M. deChoisy, commander of the French and American Forces, thus ending British rule in America. Courtesy of the Gloucester-Mathews Gazette-Journal

C. David Burke was presented with a citation by William Whitley, county administrator, for his outstanding services to the county and to the Bicentennials of '76 and '81. Burke was a long time treasurer of the county and an active member of the Bicentennial Committees. Courtesy of the Gloucester-Mathews Gazette-Journal

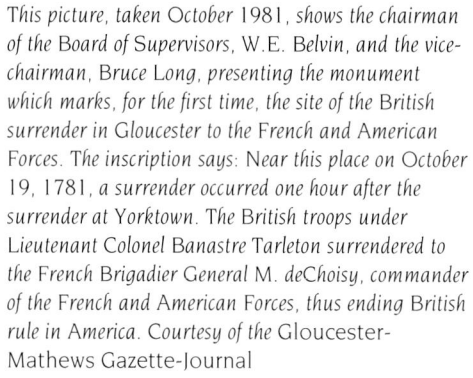

Bicentennial Farm Certificate

Virginia

Presented by

Virginia Farm Bureau Federation

Recognition is extended to those who possessed the forethought and economic ability to preserve the family ownership of this farm for 200 years or more.

This is to certify that the farm in possession of

LT. COL. CECIL WRAY PAGE, JR. AND MRS. ROBERT D. ALDRICH

is qualified for listing as a Bicentennial Farm

President

1979
Date issued

Secretary

This certificate honors Shelly, owned and farmed by the Pages for more than two hundred years. Courtesy of Cecil W. Page

Shelly is listed as an Historical Archaeological District by both Virginia and National Landmarks. A three-year archaeological investigation found evidence of human habitation dating to three thousand B.C. at Shelly. The artifacts found and the huge collection of shells indicate continuous occupation over many years. Both Shelly, across Carter's Creek and on the York River, and Rosewell, in the foreground, were part of the Menefee grant of 1639. Mann Page III built the first known home on Shelly in 1788. It was destroyed by fire in 1883 and rebuilt on the same foundations. It has again been rebuilt on the original foundations by the present Page owner. Shelly is renowned for its huge growth of boxwood and for its commanding view of the York River. *Courtesy of the Virginia Department of Historic Resources*

Dedication of Waterman's Hall, June 29, 1984. The speaker, Governor Charles S. Robb, had an excellent view of the York River and the beach and water facilities of the Virginia Institute of Marine Science. This building was a welcome addition to the originally meagre facilities of the Institute. It was delayed because of extensive archaeology on the property and the discovery of significant foundations of colonial Gloucester Town. The area is now recognized, and to an extent protected, as a Historical Archaeological District. *Courtesy of the Virginia Institute of Marine Science*

Cypress Manor, a well-built home on the Gloucester bank of the York River was to become the largest portion of the Watermen's Museum in Yorktown. This technological maneuver, contracted to Expert Housemovers of Virginia Beach, attracted much interest and many observers. The effort was the victim of a falling tide and the manor spent the night on the north shore but crossed the York successfully on high tide the next day. Courtesy of the Watermen's Museum, Yorktown

Holly Knoll, now listed on Virginia and National Landmarks, is the central building of the Moton Conference Center and was the Gloucester home of Dr. Robert R. Moton. Dr. Moton, a native Virginian, followed Booker T. Washington as president of Tuskegee. After a distinguished career he retired to Cappahosic and built his home on the York River. It is now the nucleus of a center for educational conferences of great variety and distinction. *Courtesy of the Moton Conference Center*

Dr. Moton with two of his associates at Tuskegee. Left to right are Booker T. Washington's secretary Emmett Scott, Dr. Robert R. Moton, and Booker T. Washington. *Courtesy of the Gloucester-Mathews Gazette-Journal*

These two sheriffs of Gloucester County, father and son, lived at "Waonda" near Gloucester Court House.

Eugene P. Rhodes and his wife, Charlotte Selden, bought the place when Sinclair, the third son, was about two years old.

They moved there from Point Lookout, then called Cloverfield. Eugene was Sheriff from 1935 until he retired December 31, 1955. G. Sinclair Rhodes served as deputy in 1966 to 1975 and as sheriff from 1975 until his retirement in 1979. Another son, Lee F. Rhodes, was deputy for seven years. This makes a total of forty years of Gloucester sheriffcy in this one family. It is interesting that Eugene's father was also a sheriff. He served in Texas in the early days and was killed in the line of duty—but that is another story. Courtesy of Merwyn Rhodes and Mary Sinclair Rust

Tractors were used more than mules but Billy Gray sometimes used oxen for hauling and fun! Courtesy of Elizabeth R. Gray

Daffodils are still sold on roadsides by the bunch—sometimes! Courtesy of the Gloucester-Mathews Gazette-Journal

157

W.N. Gray and his four sons are setting out pine seedlings, 1953. In more recent times this is usually done in large areas by machinery. Courtesy of Elizabeth R. Gray

Lamberth Building Supplies is now operated by a daughter, Agnes Hogge, and other relatives of George Lamberth (in a blue shirt looking up at the new structure). He rebuilt his plant and his business after a disastrous fire. Long associated with timber, lumber and building materials, the Lamberths dispensed building supplies and building advice to Gloucester people. George Lamberth was a craftsman as well as a businessman. He loved to do a challenging piece of work himself—and always did it well. Courtesy of Margaret Lamberth

Herbert I. Lewis, son of the founder and first president, Marshall Lewis, was also president of the Bank of Gloucester. He will be long remembered as a banker but also as a benefactor for many projects in the county. After the Lewis regime the bank joined the United Virginia Bank which has now taken the name Crestar. The bank still stands, as it always has, on Main Street, Gloucester. There is a branch on Route 17, south. Courtesy of the Daily Press

This picture and the one on the following pages show oysters and fish being processed at the old oyster house on Whittakers Creek, off the Severn River. This seafood business was operated by the Sterlings for two or three generations and more recently under the ownership of Col. Wyatt Carneal. It is now closed. Courtesy of Wyatt B. Carneal, Jr.

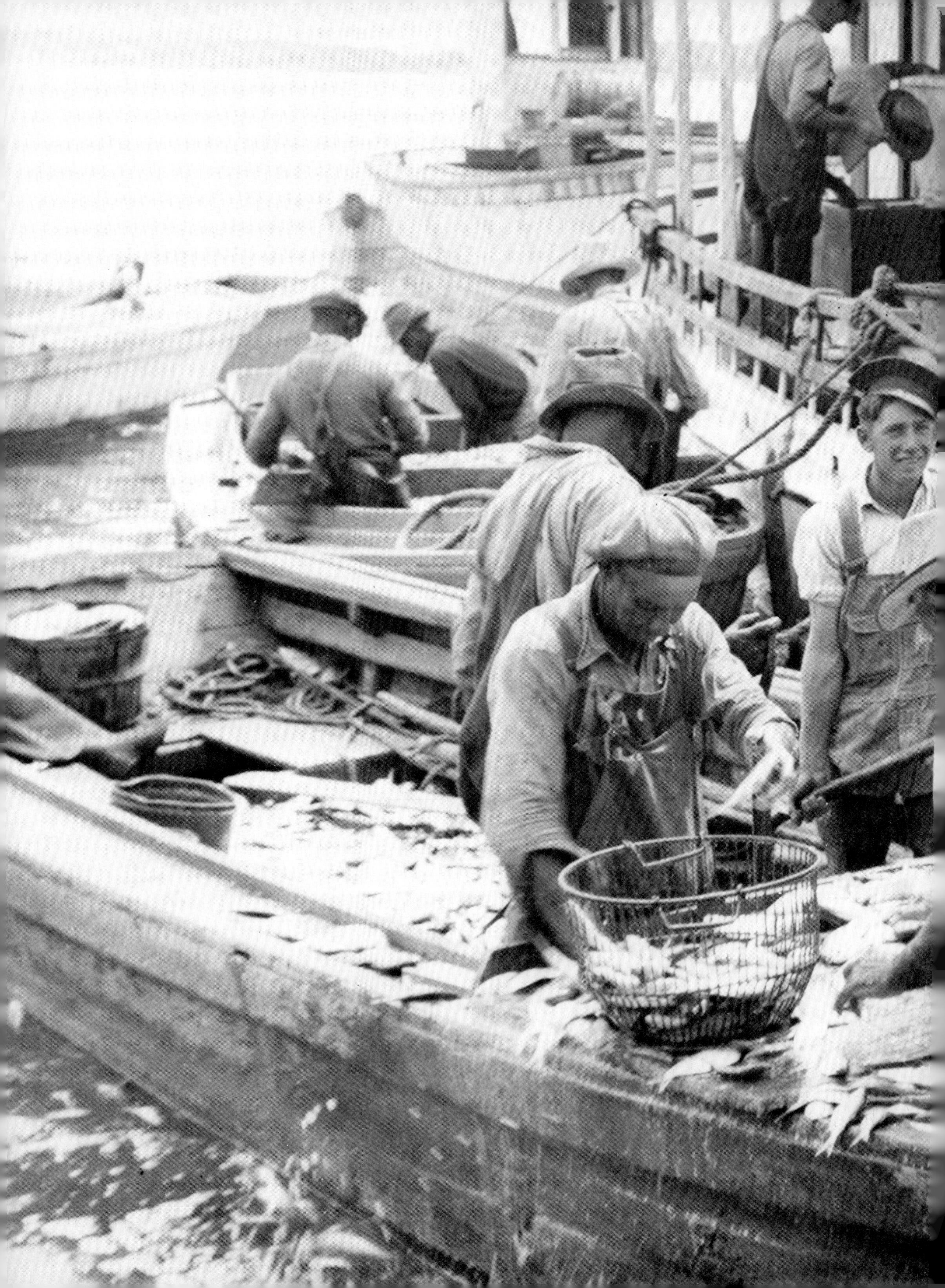

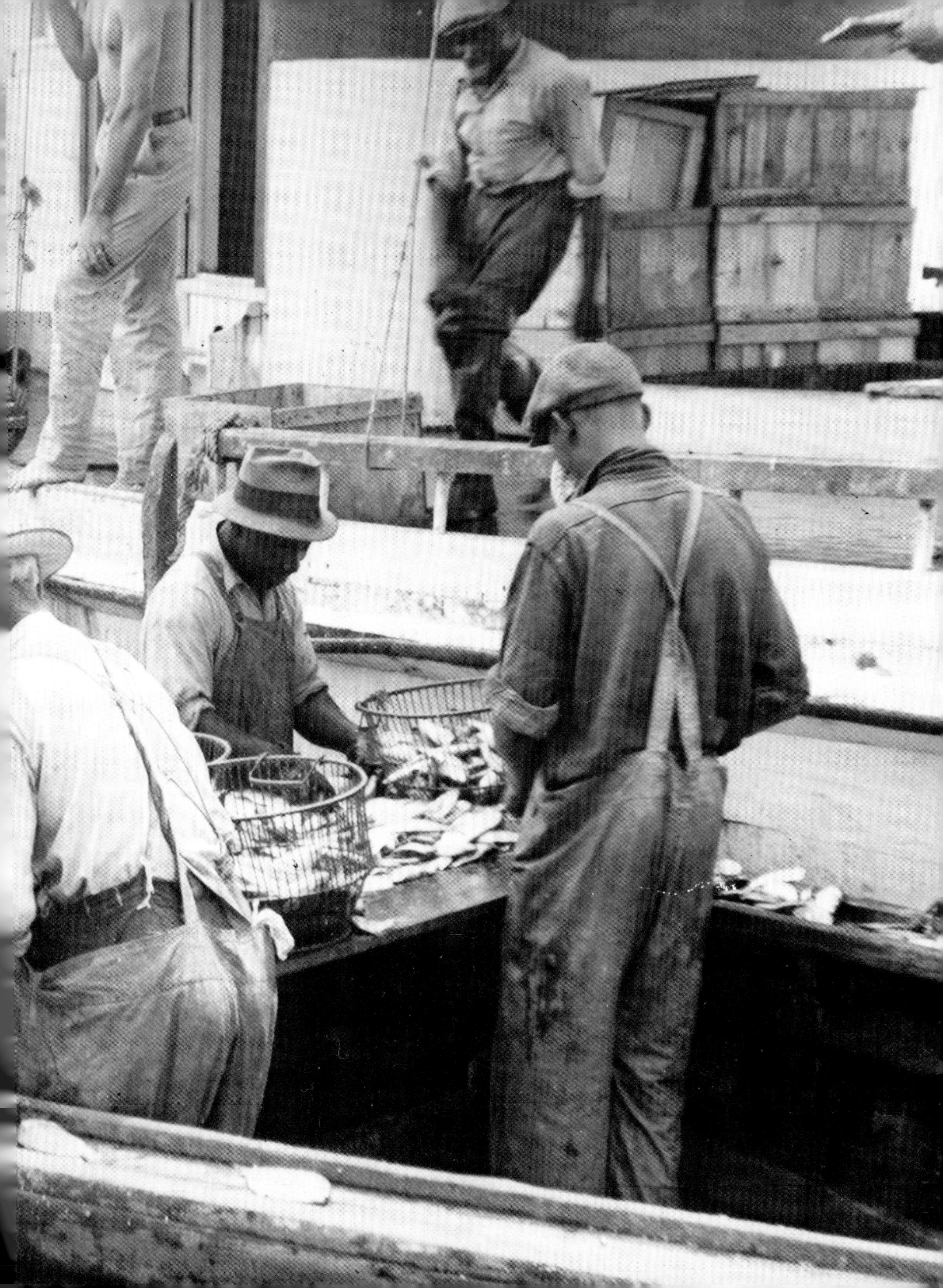

Basil Bernard Roane was deputy and clerk of the circuit court for fifty-nine years. In April 1976, the clerk's office, built in 1896, was named for him. It is the building in which he spent most of his career. It has recently been designated as a museum for the county.
Courtesy of the Daily Press

John Warren Cooke, longtime member and Speaker of the House of Representatives, was also owner and editor of the Gloucester-Mathews Gazette-Journal. He has now been succeeded as editor by his daughter, Elsa, but he is still active in the publishing business. Mr. Cooke's influence in the General Assembly and as a publisher has been incalculable. He is sadly missed in Richmond. This picture shows him at the Speaker's desk. Courtesy of the Daily Press

Trash disposal is a cumulative problem in Gloucester as elsewhere. This scene at the Landfill tells the story. In 1986 the county procured a wood waste incinerator to help the situation. The Supervisors have sought and are still seeking better methods of waste disposal. Courtesy of the Gloucester-Mathews Gazette-Journal

As Gloucester's population has grown so has the need for services. There are now two well-organized Volunteer Fire Departments in the county: Gloucester, with a branch at Harcum, and Abingdon. This picture was taken of the Cothren home at Bellamy as firemen tried to reach a fire on the roof. Courtesy of the Gloucester-Mathews Gazette-Journal

163

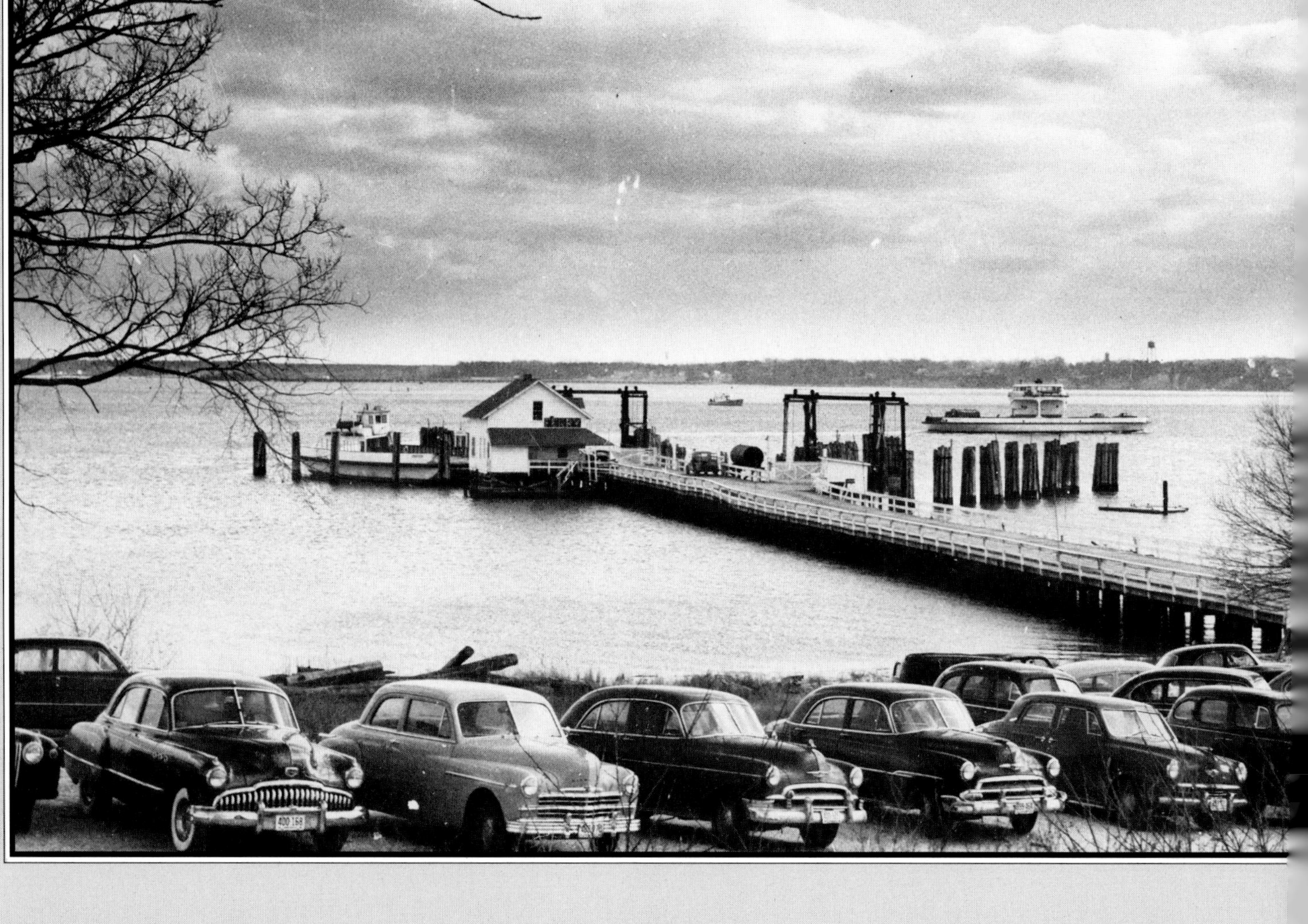

CHAPTER EIGHT
Gloucester's Special Characteristics

Introduction

This eighth and final chapter does not follow the chronological order of the other seven. Instead, it is intended to emphasize to the reader those characteristics which seem always to have given to Gloucester County its unique character and special charm. Its focus is on children, the peace of large vistas, the beauty of flowers, woods and water, the pleasure and fun of utilizing the out-of-doors, the hospitality of large homes, and the glory of good food. In this chapter are gathered pictures of places and events which Gloucester people cherish and which attract an ever-growing population.

If pictures are from the Sinclair collection credit is not acknowledged but assumed.

The old ferry dock with the first large ferry, the Cornwallis, *approaching—and cloud formations above the York River, circa 1950. Courtesy of the Daily Press*

165

Old House Creek shimmers through the trees on Sherwood's lawn. Courtesy of Donald R. Perritt

Abundant grass and large trees offer good grazing and deep shade on Gloucester farms. Courtesy of Donald R. Perritt

Wrought-iron gates opened to Sherwood's garden where early planted shrubs have grown to trees. Courtesy of Donald R. Perritt

Post and rail fence on pond. Courtesy of the Gloucester Historical Committee

This weather-beaten barn once processed tobacco; now it is used for daffodils on the Heath property. Courtesy of the Gloucester Historical Committee

Virginia's most historic ruin is Rosewell, owned and preserved by the Gloucester Historical Society, managed and funded by Rosewell Foundation. This picture shows the wonderfully preserved wine cellar and the beautiful brickwork of the mid-eighteenth century.

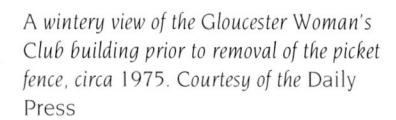

A wintery view of the Gloucester Woman's Club building prior to removal of the picket fence, circa 1975. Courtesy of the Daily Press

Dragon Run in winter. Courtesy of the Daily Press

With winter's embellishments.

Bits of Gloucester's Architecture

Gloucester, as one of the older counties, has a surprising number of original colonial buildings: Abingdon and Ware Churches, Seawell's and Long Bridge (Edge Hill) Ordinaries, Botetourt Building (Botetourt Tavern), and the Colonial Court House are well-authenticated, eighteenth-century public buildings. Five homes standing from the seventeenth century have been well documented—Abingdon Glebe, Free School House, Lowland Cottage, Toddsbury, and Mount Prodigal. There may be, and probably are, others but records are missing. There are many eighteenth-century homes in the county and of a great variety of size, beauty, and structure. Virginia and National Landmarks Registers have cited twenty-two sites in the county. A Works Progress Administration survey listed ninety-seven.

Many of Gloucester's homes and buildings are pictured throughout this volume; others or different photographs are added here to show special features or views. This is not intended to portray an architectural survey of the county but to suggest that Gloucester has an historic architectural wealth as yet unrecognized and unexplored.

Local Sites On The Virginia Landmarks Register for Gloucester

Abingdon Episcopal Church
Abingdon Glebe House
Airville
Burgh Westra
Fairfield Archaeological Site
Gloucester Court House Historic District
Gloucester Point Archaeological District
Gloucester Woman's Club (Long Bridge Ordinary)
Holly Knoll
Kempsville
Land's End
Little England
Lowland Cottage
Roaring Springs
Rosewell
Shelly
Timberneck
Toddsbury
Walter Reed's Birthplace
Ware Episcopal Church
Warner Hall
White Hall
Courtesy of the Gloucester-Mathews Gazette-Journal

Severn Lodge's yard is almost in the water of Severn River. Courtesy of the Gloucester Historical Committee

173

Airville, the home of John Dixon of Dixon's Light Horse Cavalry in the Revolution, and his parents, was built circa 1756 and had a large wing added later. Its special feature is the unusual hanging staircase. Courtesy of Gloucester Historical Committee

Courtesy of the Gloucester-Mathews Gazette-Journal

174

Belle Ville, graciously enlarged over the years, was built about 1658 by John Curtis. It was acquired about fifty years later by the Booths and remained in the Booth-Taliaferro family until recent years. Courtesy of the Gloucester Historical Committee

Burgh Westra, on the North River, is named for the Scottish home of which it is a copy. It was built in 1855 by Warner Taliaferro for his son, Phillip, who was then studying medicine in Edinburgh. The architecture is unique in Gloucester. "Doctor Phil" set up a hospital in the house during the Civil War. Burgh Westra has remained in the Taliaferro family but suffered a disastrous fire in 1988 and has been meticulously rebuilt. Courtesy of the Gloucester Historical Committee

Cherokee was constructed as a twentieth century addition to an eighteenth century ice house on Exchange. This unusual adaptation has made a comfortable and picturesque home. Courtesy of the Gloucester Historical Committee

Elmington has more beauty and magnificence to offer than this imposing Greek Revival entrance. The colonial Whiting home was replaced by this building attributed to Dr. John Prosser Tabb circa 1850. It was altered significantly by Thomas Dixon when he lived there in the early years of this century. Courtesy of the Glousester Historical Committee; photo by Bob Marble.

Glen Roy stands high above the Ware River and may be seen from the river's far side. It is a square-built house of 1850, by William Patterson Smith, with roof railings reminiscent of New England. Courtesy of the Gloucester Historical Committee; photo by Bob Bailey

Goshen, an early Tomkies estate, was a Perrin home for nearly two hundred years. Like many Tidewater homes it has two fronts, one on the water and another for arriving visitors. Goshen also has a modern saltwater pool. Courtesy of the Gloucester Historical Committee; photo by Bob Bailey

*This partially
buried round ice
house at Hockley
(visible to the right) is
typical of those built in Gloucester
on the early plantations. This round style is
said to be unique; several remain in the county.
Courtesy of the Gloucester Historical Committee; photo by Bob Bailey*

From Land's End can be seen both branches of the Severn River and out to the Mobjack Bay. Built by Captain John Sinclair in the late eighteenth century it was restored by the Lancianos in the 1960s. At this time the ballroom, a one-story wing (Cary Jones, circa 1830) was replaced by a three-story brick addition. The Dutch gambrel roof and several indoor features are unique and original. Photo by Bailey and Biggs Studio

Purton, an early home on the York River, dating to 1650, has been rebuilt and since has had several harmonious additions. It is now a modern home with spacious grounds. Courtesy of the Gloucester Historical Society

This welcome to Gloucester County and to White Marsh Plantation was written by H.N. Bee, who at that time lived at White Marsh. It was published in a small pamphlet "Courtesy of Gloucester-Yorktown Ferry" called Historic Tidewater Virginia: White Marsh Plantation.

Dear Stranger:

You are about to land on the shores of Gloucester County, Virginia. Gloucester County with its adjoining county, Mathews, is the very center of Tidewater Virginia. You can not know this beautiful section from its fine highways, you do not see the old homes, and the unusual shore lines, and appreciate the call of this glorious county. Glorious in history, inspiring in romance, and unforgettable in its sports and pastimes.

In this section of our country, the United States was born. Then there were no roads, the homes were all built on the shore lines of the rivers and bays. So many are disappointed as they traverse our fine highways and see nothing but filling stations, homes of the business element, and the colored folks; the one exception is, as they pass from one county to another they reach the county seats, small settlements, but rich in atmosphere and history, all built in the early years of our great nation. I do not want you to journey through and be disillusioned, it is not fair to you or Historic Tidewater Virginia. Off the highway, if you only knew, are places well worth pausing to see. You will not regret your stop.

You are cordially invited to drive into White Marsh Plantation, the entrance is on the highway, half way between the Yorktown Ferry and Gloucester Court House. There you will get an impression of one of our old homes. Drive down the avenue, nearly a mile, until you reach the circle in front of the old Mansion, park your car on the road to the right and walk around the grounds. Should I have the pleasure of seeing you I could tell you something of Historic Tidewater Virginia, that you will carry away with you some of the enthusiasm we feel, that you may understand why we believe ours is a blessed lot, privileged to live in this land of history, romance and unexcelled climate, yet unspoiled, where depression is seldom known, surrounded by descendants of the old families of Virginia, where hostility is never known, and hospitality is ever shown.

Respectfully,
H.N. Bee
Courtesy of C. David Burke

Abingdon Church with its Christmas wreaths. Having suffered the ravages of time and two wars the interior was recently restored. The exterior is almost as it was in colonial times. Courtesy of Abingdon Church

Dogwood at the entrance of the Court House Green. Courtesy of the Gloucester Historical Committee

Children, our insurance for the future

Lewis Avenue was never the same after the Kerns' children moved away and took their ponies with them.

Heather tends a baby goat—two kids together!

Top photo: The "littlest ones" socialize in the yard at Bay Cottage in Robins Neck. Bottom Photo: Sheriff Sinclair Rhodes takes his grandchildren and their friends crabbing at Warehouse Landing. Courtesy of Merwyn Rhodes

Jeff Sinclair, Jr., and Eugene Rhodes consider crabbing.

A solemn seashore consultation.

Andrew Corr has a birthday party at his grandfather's Roadview Farm. Andrew is on the pony in front. Photos by Jean Corr

Gloucester's waterways offer recreation, food, employment and remarkable beauty.

Sails coming from Ware River Yacht Club into the Mobjack Bay. Courtesy of Deborah Kerns Anderson

Bay Eagle from VIMS on a scientific excursion near the mouth of the York River. Courtesy of the Virginia Institute of Marine Science

The loftiness of the Coleman Bridge with a huddle of small craft passing under it —a beautiful day. Courtesy of the Watermen's Museum, Yorktown

Flood tide, fall of 1974, on Caucas Bay.

The schooner Edward L. Martin in Wilson's Creek. Courtesy of the Watermen's Museum, Yorktown

Sailfish sailing off Four Point Marsh. Courtesy of Merwyn Rhodes

Canoeing on Back Creek. Courtesy of Merwyn Rhodes

Swans visit Free School Creek, winter 1989. Courtesy of Mrs. Samuel Deal

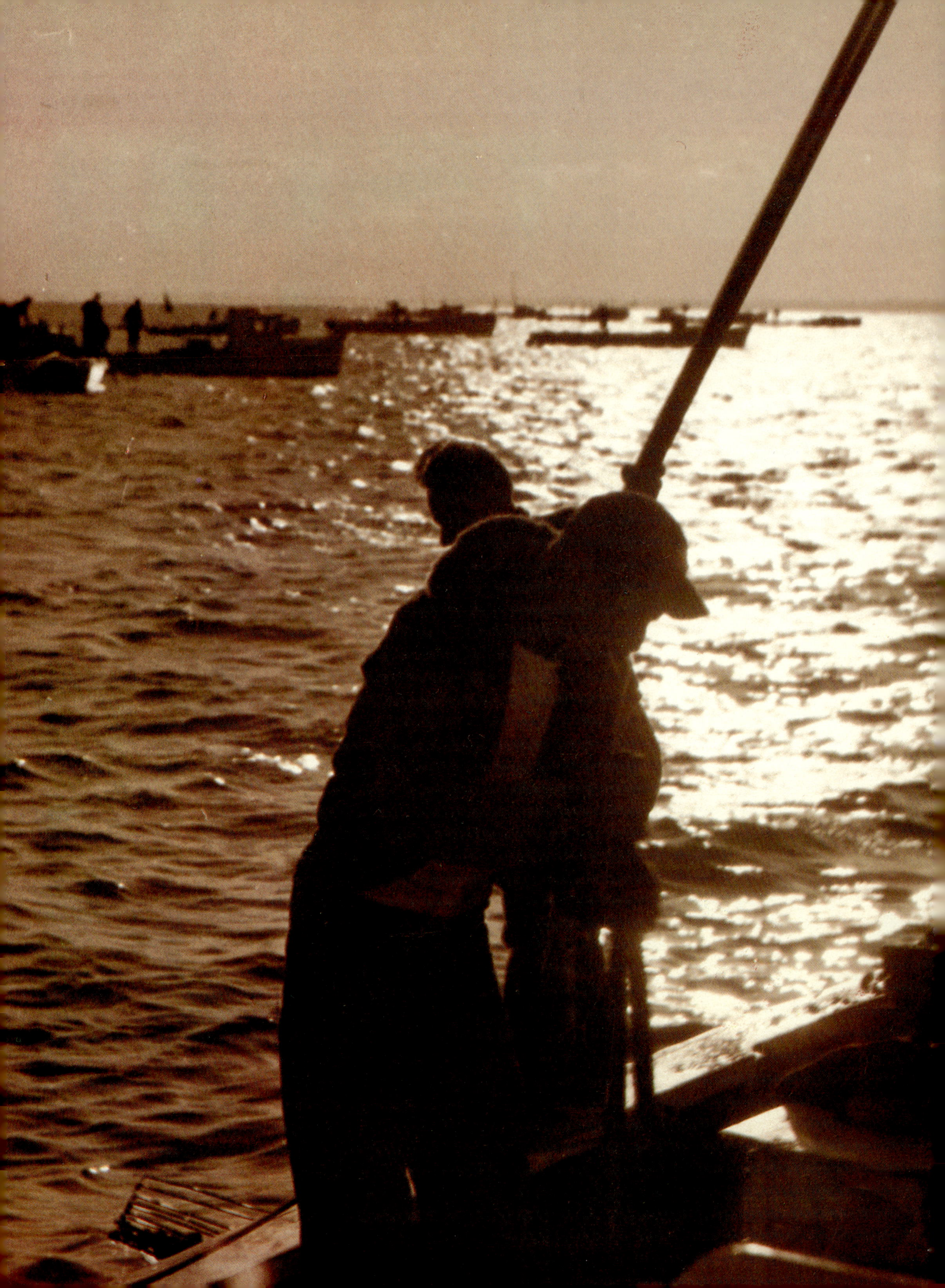

Working on the water at this hour is an artistic experience. Courtesy of the Daily Press

Horses and Hounds

Fox hunting has a drama which has appealed in Gloucester since the early 1700s. It is practiced here by hunters in trucks and hunters on horses, by men and women in traditional pink and black coats and by others in jeans and "what have you." In these four pictures, the Sinclairs show the two styles. The persons pictured and the horses and hounds are descendants of those who survived the Civil War in the Confederate Army and at Marlfield in Gloucester. The horn which Wythe Sinclair is using was his grandfather's.

Sinclairs, horses and hounds descended from the survivors of the Civil War; in traditional garb and with traditional horns.

But they hunt in modern cross-country style with trucks too.

Ring, of the noble head, is the proud product of generations of careful breeding.

Wythe is using his grandfather's horn. Bound in silver, it has announced and terminated fox hunts in Gloucester for more than one hundred years.

The James River Hunt finds its regular hunting grounds in Gloucester. Alex Wiatt and Phil Stafford on Big Daddy and Fly Boy lead the hunt to the cast at Shelly, circa 1974. Courtesy of S.P. Stafford

The beautiful Kerns Trophy is awarded for the first time and won by Norma Jean Kerns on Humdinger, owned by Indie L. Sinclair.

A few years later Charles Kerns, Sr. the donor of the trophy, presented it to Joy Goodson who won it at the Gloucester Horse and Pony Club Show on the grounds of the Gloucester Day School (now Ware Academy) 1974. Courtesy of Charles J. Kerns

Beauty in the Countryside
Flowers, Gardens and Yards

Gloucester is known for its daffodils - they naturalize and make their own beauty spots. Courtesy of Carol Ray

Planted and cultivated in large fields daffodils contribute to the economy. Courtesy of Carol Ray

Closeups reveal marvels of symmetry and color. Courtesy of Carol Ray

What bluebird could resist this home on North River? Courtesy of Carol Ray

197

Daffodils at Toddsbury flash a golden signal of Spring. Begun by Thomas Todd about 1650, this Gloucester County home still shelters a Todd descendant, Mrs. Gordon Bolitho (left), together with her husband (right). North River shows through the ancient elms and oaks. Photo by Howell Walker, copyright © April 1956 by National Geographic Society

Spring enhances the beauty of the Lisburne Gardens. Courtesy of Mrs. David L. Peebles

The pond area at Lisburne is beautiful at all seasons. Courtesy of Mrs. David L. Peebles

The spring for which Roaring Springs is named. It no longer roars but enhances the beauty of the lawn.

The Christmas Tree Lighting: *The neighborliness which is typical of Gloucester County is epitomized by the Christmas Tree Lighting which Elsie and Tommy Dame of the Homeplace in Robins' Neck have offered the community for the past ten years. The cedar tree, now about thirty-five feet tall and beautifully shaped, "just grew up" in one of the flower beds about thirty years ago. Mrs. Dame immediately accepted it as the outdoor Christmas tree she had always wanted. She saw it as a symbol of Christmas which would give joy to all who came to her home and also those who passed it by. So the tree grew and every year the Dames and the Gwyns added more lights to the tree and putting on the lights became an occasion for a family gathering and a series of events. Getting the lights and checking them, choosing the dates for putting on the lights, lighting the tree—all of this must be done well in advance of December 25 so that everyone could enjoy the lighted tree throughout the Christmas season. The Gwyns (Elsie Dame was born a Gwyn) are a large family and a close one. As they gathered each Christmas and the six Dame children grew and married there were many little ones; they were joined by friends and relatives and gradually the Dame's Tree Lighting became a Christmas tradition and an occasion for the whole neighborhood, indeed for the county. Here at the Homeplace hundreds of people gather every December. There is a mystery as they converge silently upon the huge tree and then wonder and ecstasy as every light on the tree comes on. The occasion is solemnized by religious music and readings and special joy is given the children when Santa Claus appears on the roof and descends to talk with them. Refreshments are available in a nearby building. The spirit of Christmas is abroad and everyone is grateful to the Dames for offering this beautiful beginning to the blessed season.*

Courtesy of Dottie Dame Hogge

BIBLIOGRAPHY

A Flag for Gloucester County! Several flags have been designed for special occasions and events but this one, carefully stitched and designed under the auspices of the Gloucester Historical Committee, was adopted by the Board of Supervisors for the county in November 1989. It is presented here in its beautiful colors.

Abingdon Church. *The Way We Are.* White Marsh, Va.: Abingdon Church, 1979.

Association for Preservation of Virginia Antiquities. *Preserving Virginia, 1889–1989.* Centennial Pictorial designed and produced by Art Bank, Virginia, 1989.

Bodie, Charles A. and William A. Siener for the Gloucester Historical Committee. *A Guide to Gloucester County, Virginia Historical Manuscripts, 1651-1865.* Richmond: Virginia State Library, 1976.

Bowman, Clementine R. "The Fox Hunting Sinclairs." *The Hunters Horn.* December 1974: Cover and p. 9.

Bowman, Clementine Rhodes. *Gloucester County, Virginia: A History.* Verona, Va.: McClure Printing Co., 1982.

Bulletin of the Gloucester Historical Society in Virginia. Vol. 1, Nos. 2 and 6, Gloucester, Va.

Burwell, George Harrison. *Record of the Burwell Family.* Richmond: Whittet and Shepperson, 1908.

Chowning, Larry S. *Harvesting the Chesapeake: Tools and Traditions.* Centreville, Maryland: Tidewater Publishers, 1990.

Cometti, Elizabeth. *Social Life in Virginia During the War of Independence.* Williamsburg: Virginia Independence Bicentennial Commission, 1978.

Dabney, Mary Howard, compiler. ". . .Past is Prologue," *Gloucester County, Virginia.* Gloucester: Gloucester County and Gloucester County Historical and Bicentennial Committee, 1973.

Dabney, Virginius. *Virginia: The New Dominion.* Garden City, NY: Doubleday and Co., 1971.

Dixon, Marion O. "History of Gloucester-Yorktown Ferry System 1864-1952." Research paper, Old Dominion University, 1987.

Dixon, Thomas, Jr. *The Life Worth Living: A Personal Experience.* New York: Doubleday, Page & Company, 1905.

Fauber Garbee, Inc., Architects. *Court Green and Botetourt Building: Feasibility Study.* Gloucester County, Va., 1979.

Garnett, David. *Pocahontas.* New York: Harcourt, Brace and Company, 1933.

Gloucester County and the Gloucester Historical Committee. *Gloucester County, Virginia, Landmarks.* Newport News, Va.: Prestige Press, 1983.

Gloucester County, Virginia. *A Bicentennial Perspective.* Gloucester '76 Celebration, Inc., August 1976.

Gloucester Historical Committee. *Points and Events of Interest,* Gloucester, Va., 1990.

Gloucester Historical Committee, compilers. *Six Periods in the History of Gloucester County.* Gloucester, Va.: DeHardit Press, 1971.

Gray, Mary Wiatt. *Gloucester County (Virginia).* Richmond: Cattrell and Cooke, Inc., 1936.

Hartwell, Henry, James Blair, and Edward Chilton. *The Present State of Virginia and the College,* edited by Hunter Farish. First printed in London in 1727. Charlottesville: Dominion Books, 1964.

Joseph Bryan Branch, Association for the Preservation of Virginia Antiquities, et. al., compilers. *Epitaphs of Gloucester and Mathews Counties through 1865.* Richmond: The Virginia State Library, 1959.

Lanciano, Claude O. *Captain John Sinclair of Virginia.* Gloucester, Va.: Lands End Books, 1973.

Lanciano, Claude O. *Rosewell: Garland of Virginia.* Gloucester, Va.: Historical and Bicentennial Committee, 1978. Printed by the Delmar Co., Charlotte, N.C.

Lewis, Elizabeth Dutton and Daniel Webster Deal. *A Chronology of Gloucester County, Virginia, 1607-1790.* Prepared for the Gloucester Historical and Bicentennial Committee, Gloucester, Va., 1976.

Lewis, Elizabeth Dutton. *Revolutionary War Roster.* Gloucester County, Va.: Gloucester County and the Historical and Bicentennial Committee, 1976.

Mason, Polly Cary, compiler. *Records of Colonial Gloucester County, Virginia,* 2 vols. (1946 and 1948). Reprint (2 vols. in one), Berryville, Va.: Chesapeake Book Co., 1965-1966.

McIlwain, H.L., editor. Official Letters of the Governors of the State of Virginia. Vol. 1 ("The Letters of Patrick Henry"), pp. 11-12.

Montague, Ludwell Lee. *Gloucester County in the Civil War.* Gloucester, Va.: The DeHardit Press, 1965.

O'Neal, William B. *Architecture in Virginia.* New York, published for the Virginia Museum by Walker and Co., Inc., 1968.

Opperman, Anthony F. and E. Randolph Turner, III. "Gloucester County: Archaeology at Shelly," *Notes on Virginia,* No. 34, (Spring 1990): pp. 24-27, Virginia Department of Historic Resources.

Quarles, Marguerite Stuart. *Pocahontas (Bright Stream Between Two Hills).* Richmond: The Association for the Preservation of Virginia Antiquities, 1939.

Robins, Sallie Nelson. *Gloucester: One of the First Chapters of the Commonwealth of Virginia.* Richmond: West Johnson & Co., 1893.

Ray, Carol, compiler. *Wild About Daffodils: A Short History of the significance of the daffodil to Gloucester County, Virginia.* Gloucester, Va., Five River's Woman's Club, 1991.

Rouse, Park, Jr. *Virginia: The English Heritage in America.* New York: Hastings House, 1960.

Rouse, Park, Jr. "John Sinclair and Virginia's Navy." *The Iron Worker,* Vol. 39, No. 1: Lynchburg, Va., 1974.

Ryan, Joanne Wood. "Gloucester County, Virginia in the American

Revolution." Masters' Thesis, College of William and Mary, 1978.
Selby, John E. *A Chronology of Virginia and the War of Independence 1763-1783*. Charlottesville: The University Press for the Virginia Independence Bicentennial Commission, 1973.
Sellers, John R. *The Virginia Continental Line*. Williamsburg: The Virginia Independence Bicentennial Commission, 1978.
Sinclair, Caroline B. and Elizabeth Dutton Lewis. "The Court Houses of Gloucester County and Other Necessary Buildings." An unpublished manuscript.
Sinclair, Caroline B., compiler. *Abingdon Church: A Chronology of Its History, 1650-1970*. White Marsh, Va.: Abingdon Episcopal Church, 1972.
Sinclair, Caroline B. *The Four Families of Rosewell*. Virginia Beach: Grunewald and Radcliff Publishers, 1989.
Sinclair, Caroline B. *Stories of Old Gloucester*. Verona, Va.: McClure Press, 1974.
Stubbs, Dr. and Mrs. William Carter. *A History of Two Virginia Families: Thomas Baytop 1638 and John Catlett 1622*. New Orleans: published privately, 1918.
Stubbs, Dr. and Mrs. William Carter. *Two Virginia Families: Descendants of Mordicai Cooke and Thomas Booth*. New Orleans: published privately, 1925.
Swem, E.G. *Views of Yorktown and Gloucester Town, 1755*. Newport News, Va.: Mariners' Museum, 1946. Reprinted from the *Virginia Magazine of History and Biography*, Vol. 54, No. 2, 1946.
Tabb, Mary Lee. "The Gloucester Academy." Unpublished manuscript in possession of Elizabeth Harwood, Gloucester, Va.
Taylor, F.L. *A Brief Summary of the Work of Rev. William Byrd Lee in Ware, Abingdon and Adjoining Parishes, 1881-1906*. Gloucester County, Va.: Rosewell, 1906. Published privately.
Walker, Thomas Calhoun. *The Honey-Pod Tree*. New York: The John Day Co., 1958.

INDEX

A

Abingdon, 12, 18, 38, 61, 64, 163
Abingdon Church, 45, 46, 50, 60, 61, 140, 173, 182
Abingdon Church, interior, 64
Abingdon Elementary, 108
Abingdon Glebe, 29, 173
Abingdon parish, 29
Abingdon Park, 128
Achilles, 50, 69, 97, 111
Achilles High School, 97, 108, 110
Adner, 10
aeronaut, 56, 58,
Airville, 174
Alabama, 76
Anderson, Matthew, 65
Anderton, Mrs. I. M., 111
Anglican church, 12, 46
Appomattox, 59, 61
Ark, 52, 64, 137
Ark Park, 128
Arnold, Benedict, 36
Asbury, Francis, 46
Ash Wednesday high tide of 1962, 128
Ashe, Hattie, 110
Ashe, Jim, 78
Ashe, William Henry, 75, 82
Ashland, 62
Association for the Preservation of Virginia Antiquities, 124
Atlantic Fleet, 95
Aunt Jennie, 89

B

Back Creek, 189
Bacon, Nathaniel, 15, 19, 31, 45
Bacon's Rebellion, 12, 25
Baltimore, 14, 45, 74, 75
Bank of Gloucester, 74, 159
Baptist churches, 46
Battle, John S., 128
Battle of Gwyns Island, 37
Battle of the Bulge, 125
Battle of the Hook, 37
Battle of Yorktown, 38
Baulch, May, 97, 113
Bay Cottage, 46, 184
Bay Eagle, 187
Baytop Family, 27, 76
Baytop, James, 44
Baytop, Lt. William Jones, 59, 61
Beach Grove Church, 46
Beaver Dam Project, 132, 134
Beaver Dam Reservoir, 128
Bee, H. N., 181
Belcher, Mrs. E. B., 110
Bellamy, 163
Bellamy, Joseph 46, 53
Bellamy Methodist Church, 46, 53, 54
Belle Ville, 175
Belvin, W. E., 151
Bench Show, 118
Bernard, Peter, 36
Bethlehem Methodist Church, 54
Beulah Church, 46
Bicentennial, 31, 40, 109, 130, 147, 148, 150
Bicentennial Parade, 148
Black Angus, 144
Blessing of the Hounds, 138
Bluefort, Sarah, 125
Board of Supervisors, 12, 30, 73, 127, 130, 147, 148
Board of Supervisors, 151
Bohannon, Todd, 136
Bolitho, Mrs. Gordon, 198
Booth Family, 15, 26, 35, 76, 175
Booth, George, 26
Booth-Taliaferro Family, 175
Boswell, Thomas, 35
Botetourt, 29, 69, 97, 98, 107, 111, 115
Botetourt Administration Building, 13, 22, 173
Botetourt Annual, 107
Botetourt Guards, 57
Botetourt High School, 69, 110, 113, 143
Botetourt Hotel, 75
Botetourt Lodge No. 7, 41
Botetourt Tavern, 22, 32, 35, 38, 128, 173
Botetourt Town, 32
Boy Scouts, 97, 114, 115, 116
Branch of the Mayne Swampe, 25
Bridges, R. J., 71
Bristow, Marie, 110
Bristow, Robert, 28
Brown, E. D., 81
Brown, Ed, 78
Brown, Lieutenant John Thomson, 57, 71
Brown, Dr. Raymond, 133
Bryan Family, 46, 60
Bryan, Reverend Corbin Braxton, 56
Bryan, Joseph, 60
Bryan, Lieutenant John Randolph, 56, 58
Bryan, St. George Tucker Coalter, 56
Buck, Mrs. William A., 111
Buckner, Family, 15, 65
Bucker, John 26
Burgh Westra, 58, 60, 176
Burke, C. David, 151
Burke's Pond, 117
Burwell Family, 36, 140
Burwell Lewis, 36, 43
Burwell, Lewis II, 34, 36
Butts, Reverend D. G. C., 53
buy boat, 105
Byrd, Captain, 47
Byrd, Family, 140
Byrd, C.R., 71

C

Caffee, Captain, 75, 81
California, 31
Camden, 49
Camp Chesapeake, 114
Camp Fire Girls, 97, 113
Camp Hill, 96
Camp Okie, 115
Cappahosic, 27, 94, 136. 155
Cappahosic House, 27
Carmine, Walter, 124
Carneal, Col. Wyatt, 159
Carters Creek, 36
Cary, Miles, 24
Cash, 69
Catesby Field, 117
Catholic church, 46. 131
Catlett, 35
Catlett, Charles, 71
Catlett Family, 76
Catlett, John W. E. Jr., 15
Catlett, Powell, 138
Caucas Bay, 188
Cedar Hill, 75
Charles River County, 12
Cherokee, 176
Chesapeake Bay, 12, 35, 36, 104
Chief Commissioner of Virginia Naval Board, 34
Christmas Parade, 129, 142
Christmas Tree Lighting, 200
Civil War, 29, 40, 46, 51, 56, 60, 61, 176, 192
Civilian Conservation Corps, 98
Clark, Rowland, 47
Claybank, 75
Clayton, Jasper, 36
Clayton, John, 41
Clements, Margie, 111
Cloverfields, 46, 156
Coca-Cola, 97
Coleman Bridge, 49, 127, 128, 129, 188

203

College of William and Mary, 14, 129, 131
Colonial Court House, 31, 83, 173
Colonial Williamsburg, 31
Concord, 65
Confederate Monument, 13, 55, 61, 70, 71, 73
Confederate Navy, 62
Confederate Veterans, 71
Constitution of the United States, 130
Continental Lines, 37
Cook, Mildred, 111
Cooke Family, 76
Cooke, Elsa, 163
Cooke, John Warren, 163
Corbell, V.S., 71
Corbin, 140
Cornnwallis, 36, 37, 47, 55, 75, 82, 120, 165
Corr, Andrew, 186
Corr, Ethel Jones, 107
Corr, Jean, 15
Corr, Reverend Harry L.,
Corr, W.E., 74
Cothren, 163
Countrie So Faire, 151
Country Club, 98
county jail, 60
County-wide school celebration, 112
Court Day, 22, 43, 44, 73, 75
Court House Circle, 79
Court House Green, 41, 61, 73, 74, 130, 146, 182
Court House Village, 51
Courts and Office Building, 128
Cow Creek Mill, 8, 120
Cox-Lawson Family, 22
crab pots, 105
Crestar, 159
Cromwell, 15
CSS *Stonewall*, 60
Cuba, 83
Culpeper, Lord, 26
Curtis, John, 36, 175
Cypress Manor, 154

D

Dabneys, 64
Daffodil Festival, 98, 129
Daffodil Tour, 98
Daffodils, 98, 103, 129, 157, 169, 196, 198
Dame, Elsie, 200
Dame, Tommy, 200
Dangerfield, Colonel, 35
Deal, Vernetta, 69
Deal Family, 69
Deal, Knox, 96
Debtor's Prison, 20
deChoisy, General, 14, 37, 151
Declaration of Independence, 33, 130

Deep Run Hunt, 138
DeHardit, Judge John, 130
deLauzan, Duke, 36, 39
Dimmock, Blanche, 86, 91
Dimmock, Charles, 57, 58
Dimmock, Minna, 91
disestablishment, 45, 46
Dixon, John, 37, 38, 174
Dixon, Thomas, 177
Dixons Mill, 42
Dogwood, 182
Donovan, John B., 71
Dragon Run, 171
Dragon Run Festival, 130, 141
Dragon Run Float, 141
Duff, J. S.,110
Dundas, Colonel Thomas, 36
Dunham, Massie, 60
Dunmore, Governor, 34, 35
Dunmore, HMS, 35
Dunmore's defeat at Gwynn's Island, 35
Dunston, 80

E

Eagle Point, 46, 60, 138
East River, 75
Ebenezer Baptist Church, 46, 51, 125
Eddins, Samuel, 35
Edge Hill, 173
Edge Hill Ordinary, 22
Edward, L. *Martin*, 188
Edwards, Jane, 110
Elmington, 13, 60, 65, 177
Emerson, Edgar, 69
Enos, Henry, 71
Enos, L.W., 71
Episcopal church, 43
Exchange, 60, 65, 176
Expert Housemovers, 154

F

4-H Club, 97, 129
Fairfield, 36, 60
Farinholt, Robert, 97
Fary, Ada, 80
Fary, Cecil, 80
Fary, Elizabeth, 80
Fary, Emmet, 80
Fary Family, 80
Fary, Grover, 80
Fary, Hubert, 80
Fary, Joseph, 80
Fary, Lillian, 80
Fary, Marius, 80
Fary, Mrs. Marius, 80
Fary, P. T., 71
Fary, Peter, 80
Fary, Sallie, 80
Fary, Sarah (Mother), 80
Fary, W. J., 80
Fary, W. T., 80

Federal rule, 73
Field, Catesby, 117
Field, George Booth, 62
Field Trials, 118
Field, William Stephen, 62, 84
First Continental Congress, 34
First National, 76
First Presbyterian Church, 54
first shots of the war in Virginia, 58
First Virginia Infantry, 50
Fitzhugh, A. F., 71
Fitzhugh, Captain Patrick Henry, 58
Fitzhugh, Captain Thaddeus, 60
Fletcher, Wallace, 109
Folkes, R. A., 51, 61, 97, 112
Fontaine, Matthew, 36
Forest, Dennis D., 109
fort, 13, 24
Fortress Monroe, 57
Four Point Marsh, 46, 189
Fox, The Reverend John, 13
Fox, John, Jr., 22, 32, 38
Fox Mill Run, 80, 97, 148
Francis S. Sanders' Nursing Home, 128,133
Franklin, Cary, 130
Fredericksburg Lodge, 41
Free School, 67
Free School Creek, 189
Free School House, 29, 66, 173
Freeport, 75
Future Farmers, 97

G

Galveston, 61
Garden Club of Gloucester, 41
Garden Week in Virginia, 129, 140
George III, 34
Girl Scout Colonial Coast Council, 98
Girl Scout, 97, 117
Glasspiel, 121
Gleaning Baptist Church, 52
Glenns, 122
Glen Roy, 60, 78
Gloucester, 75, 123
Gloucester Academy, 66, 67
Gloucester Agricultural Fair, 76
Gloucester Bank, 73
Gloucester basketball team, 132
Gloucester Country Club, 145
Gloucester County Committee of Safety, 34, 35, 36
Gloucester County seal, 148
Gloucester Court House, 22, 122,
Gloucester Day School, 195
Gloucester Fair, 78
Gloucester First Presbyterian Church, 46
Gloucester Garden Club, 129
Gloucester Golf Courses, 145
Gloucester Grays, 58
Gloucester High School, 108, 131, 132

Gloucester Historical and Bicentennial Committee, 31, 130, 151
Gloucester Historical Museum, 147
Gloucester Historical Society, 130, 147, 170
Gloucester Horse and Pony Club, 129
Gloucester Horse and Pony Club Show, 195
Gloucester Horse Show, 139
Gloucester Hunt Club, 129
Gloucester Intermediate School, 151
Gloucester Milittia, 35, 36, 37, 38, 39, 44, 47, 55, 57
Gloucester Parks and Recreation Department, 137
Gloucester Point, 127
Gloucester Redshirts, 57
Gloucester Resolution, 34
Gloucester Token, 31
Gloucester Town, 14, 24, 37, 153
Gloucester Training School, 111
Gloucester Woman's Club, 170
Gloucester women, 61
Gloucester-Matthews Tour, 129
Gloucester-Yorktown Ferry, 82, 181
Goodson, Joy, 195
Goshen, 121, 178
graded school, 61, 112
graded system, 74
Graham, Katherine, 87
Graham, Selden, 87
Grant, General Ulysses, 60
Gravesend, 12
Gray, Billy, 136, 157
Gray, Mary Wiatt (Mrs. Russell), 113
gray cloth, 58
Gray, Mrs. William, 144
Gray Family, 68
Gray, W. N., 158
Great Depression, 98
Great Road, 36
Great Storm of August 23, 120
Greater Guinea Jubilee, 130, 146
Greater Tidewater, 98
Greaves, Lieutenant Colonel Fielding L., 130
Greaves, Nellie, 137
Greene, Michael, 137
Greene, Ronnie, 137
Greenway, 46
Groves, Julia Wharton, 107
Groves, Reverend William, 46
Groves Memorial, 46
Guinea, 15, 58, 130, 146
Gywn, Edmund, 13
Gywn Family, 200
Gywn, Hugh, 44
Gywn, Tabb, 99
Gywn's Island, 32, 35

H

Hall, Joseph, 71
Hall, Thomas, 44
Hampton, 45, 63, 81, 86, 98, 129
Hampton Institute, 74
Hampton Roads, 49, 95
Hancock, John, 33
Harcum, 52, 163
Harwood, Captain, 95
Hayes, 116, 128
Hayes, Bertha, 110
Hayes High School, 108, 111
Hayes Plaza, 130, 146
Hayes, W. R. 110
Hayes, Mrs. W. R., 110
Haynes Mill, 135
Haynes Mill Pond, 135
Hazel, 128, 135
Heath, 169
Heather, 184
Heritage Council, 98
Hickory Fork House, 66
high schools, 61, 74, 107, 112, 128
Highgate, 38
Historic Tidewater Virginia, 181
Historical And Bicentennial Committee, 130
Historical Archaeological District, 153
Hobday, Lawrence, 36
Hockley, 179
hog killing, 102
Hogg, William, 61
Hogge, Agnes, 158
Hogge, Christine, 143
Hogge, Melvin, 8
Holly Knoll, 155
Home Mission Committee of East Hanover Presbytery, 46
Homeplace, 200
Honey-pod Tree, 43, 45, 76
Hook, 37, 38, 39
Hopewell, 95
Horse Show, 118
Horsley Family, 68
hospital, 37
Hubbard, 10
Hudgins, Robert, 45
Hudson and Essex, 97
Hughes, Edward, 36
Hughes, Mr. and Mrs. George, 46, 54
Hunt Ball, 118
Huntington Library, 21

I

ice house, 176, 179
Indian artifacts, 15
Indians, Gloucester, 11
Isle of Wight, 44
Italy, 61, 62

J

Jackson, General "Stonewall", 59
jail, 73, 75
James River Hunt, 194
James River Hunt Club, 129, 138
Janney, Emily, 98
Japan, 99
Jefferson, Thomas, 37
Jennie, Aunt, 89
Jennie, Miss, 69
John Clayton Building, 41
John Clayton Natural History Society, 41
John Hudgins Property, 150
Johnson, Heywood, 109
Johnston, General Joseph E., 58, 59, 60, 61
Jones, Cary, 180
Jones, Cateby, 44, 125,
Jones, Charlie, 75
Jones Dr. F. W., 71
Jones Family, 125
Jones, Maryus, 71
Jones, Richard, 44
Jones, Rosa Folkes, 125
Jones, S. F. , 111
Jones, Sallie, 87
Jones, William ap Walker, 61
Joshua Reynolds, 37

K

Kemp, Katie, 110
Kenney Building, 29, 107
Kenney, J. W., 97
Kerns, Charles J., 79
Kerns, Charles, Sr., 195
Kerns, Marius V., 48, 119
Kerns, Norma Jean, 195
Kerns, William Vernon, 119
Kerns Trophy, 195
Kilravock, 47
King and Queen Cavalry, 58
King, Charles, 12
King James, 14
Kings Council, 34
King's Lynn Museum, 17
Kingston, 12
Kingston Parish, 12, 17, 18

L

Lafayette, General, 38, 39
Lamberth, Bates, 68
Lamberth Building Supplies, 158
Lamberth, George, 158
Lamberth, Margaret, 147
Lamberth, Marie, 68
Lancianos Family, 180
landfill, 163
Lands End, 46, 180
Langely Field Flyway, 97
last Confederate flag, 61
Lawrence, Richard, 25
Lee, Colonel, 25
Lee, Eliza, 50
Lee Family, 14
Lee, General, 61
Lee, The Reverend William Byrd, 50
Lee, Mrs. William Byrd, 50
Leeland, 50
LeGrand, Joan, 136
Level Greene, 14
Lewis Avenue, 126, 183
Lewis Family, 14, 38, 44
Lewis, General, 35
Lewis, Herbert I., 159
Lewis, John, 19, 46, 60
Lewis Marshall, 159
Lewis, Olen, 146
Lewis, Warner, 35, 36, 43
Lewis's Roster, 37
Light Dragoons, 58
Lilly, Captain Thomas, 36
Lincoln, General, 37
Lincoln, President, 57
Lions Club, 129, 146
Lisburne, 199
Lisburne Gardens, 198
Little England, 37, 40
Little Richmond, 75
Long Bridge, 173
Long Bridge Ordinary, 22
Long, Bruce, 151
Lowland Cottage, 28, 173,
Luxembourg, 125

M

Magruder, General, 61
Main Road to the Dragon Bridge, 25
Main Street, 74
Manarin, Dr. Louis, 131
Mann, John, 13
Mann Family, 35
Marinas, 106
Marlfield, 15, 26, 46, 60, 63, 192
Martin School, 68
Martin's store, 74
Maryus, 78
Mason, Fred J., 117
Mason, Wilbur, 71
Masonic Building, 41
massacre, 12, 13
Mathews County, 12, 18, 41, 81, 131, 181
Mathews Court House, 17
Mathews, General Thomas, 17
Mattapony Path, 25
May Day, 111, 143
Maury, Matthew Fontaine, 36
McClellan, 58
McColley, Robert, 74
McKee, Miss, 93
Meeting House Corner, 45, 46
Memorial Church, 54
Menefee, George, 13
Menefee, Grant, 13
Mermaid, 139
Methodist churches, 46
Middle Peninsula, 49
Middlesex County, 131
Midgett, Henry, 114
Mill, 42, 75
Minor, Ruth, 107
Mobjack, 75, 81
Mobjack Bay, 36, 44, 75, 98, 104, 180, 187
Moore, Pearl, 110
Moore, Thomas, 71
Moorman, Roger, 106
Morck, Wesley, 133
Morgan, James, 148
Morgan, Dr. L. V., 133
Mosby, Colonel John S., 60
Mosquito control, 132
Moton Conference Center, 155
Moton, Dr. Robert R., 155
Mount Prodigal, 10, 173
Mount Vernon, 38
Mount Zion Methodist Church, 53
Mueller, The Reverend Howard, 138
Mumfort View 4-H Club, 116

Cook's Landing. Courtesy of B. L. Walton, Jr.

205

A typical Guinea Marsh. Courtesy of B. L. Walton, Jr.

museum, 130, 162

N

National Landmark, 29, 36, 153, 155, 173
National Register of Historic Places, 28
Naxera, 46, 55, 77, 96
New, John, 32, 35
New Orleans, 76
New York, 43, 74
Newcomb, Mary Annie, 107
Newington Baptist Church, 51
Newport News, 81, 98, 133
Noland, Elizabeth, 87
Norfolk, 17, 58, 75, 81
Norfolk, England, 17
North River, 12, 36, 65, 75, 176, 197, 198
Numismatic Collection of Johns Hopkins University, 31

O

Oakland-Pontiac agency, 72
official state dog, 137
O'Hare, General, 37
Ohio, 58
Old House Creek, 166
Opecancanough, 11
Ordinary, 39, 51, 128
Otter, HMS, 35
Owsley, Jim, 147
oxen, 100, 157

P

Page, Captain Thomas Jefferson, 60, 62
Page, Colonel Powhatan, 61
Page Family, 44, 152
Page home, 36
Page John, 33, 34, 35, 36, 43
Page, John of North End, 34
Page, Judith Burwell, 36
Page, Major, 59
Page, Colonel Powhatan Robertson, 58, 59, 61
Page, Mann I, 35
Page, Mann II, 35
Page, Mann III, 153
Page, Mary Mann, 13
Page Middle School, 131
Page Richard M., 71, 96
Page Rock Light, 121
Page, Thomas Jefferson, 62
Paradise, 25
Parks, Jane, 47
Parliament, 34
Parrot rifle, 65
partisan companies, 59
Patrick Henry's illness, 34
Patterson, William Smith, 178
Pearl Harbor, 99
Peasley, Henry, 29
Peasley property, 66
Peninsula, 58, 75, 127, 131
Penniman, 95
Perrin, 78, 178
Perrin Creek, 81
Perrin, Eleanor, 121
Perrin Family, 121
Perrin, Thomas, 40
Perrin, W. K., 71
Persian Gulf War, 127
Petsworth, 12
Petsworth Church, 46
Petsworth District, 45
Petsworth Episcopal Church, 45
Petsworth Parrish, 15
Peyton, Sir John, 36, 38
Philadelphia, 14, 34, 43, 74
Phillip, Dr., 58
Philpotts, J. L., 71
Piankatank, 35, 44, 75
Piankatank River, 12, 35
plantation schools, 43
Plat of 1754, 20
Plat of 1769, 13, 20
Plat of 1774, 21
Plummer, Mary, 110
Pocahontas, 11, 12, 16, 17
Pocahontas Garage, 72
Point Lookout, 14, 40, 156
Pointer, A. M., 71
Pointer, Edgar, 133
population, 44, 76, 127, 132, 134, 163
Poropotank, 15, 26,
Poropotank Creek, 25, 26
Powder Horn, 34
Powers, Everett, 125
Powers, Malvin, 102
Powhatan, 11, 12, 14, 124
Powhatan's Chimney, 11, 124
Presbyterian church, 46
President of Tuskagee, 155
Princeton, 14
printing press, 26
private schools, 43, 61
Providence Baptist Church, 46, 51
Public Health Department, 98
public school, 29, 45, 61, 68, 73
pulp mill, 103
Purton, 11, 181

R

Raines, Cora, 107
Randolph, John, 60
Randolph-Macon College, 60
Rappahannock, 131
Rappahannock Community College, 130, 131, 141
Rappahannock Road Path, 25
Reconstruction, 61, 98
Recreation Department, 128
Reed, Walter, 76, 83
religious faith, 51
religious instruction, 43
religious life, 45, 46, 131
Revolutionary War, 13, 24, 35, 40, 42 ,60
Rhodes, Charlotte Selden, 156
Rhodes, Eugene, 77
Rhodes, Lee F., 156
Rhodes, Marion, 87
Rhodes, Merwyn, 142
Rhodes, Robert G., 77, 185
Rhodes, Sinclair, 142, 156, 184
Rich, Everett, 150
Richmond, 12, 43, 58, 59, 60, 75, 131, 144
Rilee, Richard, 64
Ring, 193
Riverside, 47, 133
Riverside Hospital, 128
Riverside Walter Reed Hospital, 128, 133
Roadview Farm, 186
Roane, Basil Bernard, 12, 162
Roane Building, 130, 147
Roane, Charles, 10
Roane, Henley, 69
Roanes Family, 52
Roaring Springs, 62, 199
Robb, Governor Charles S., 153
Roberts, P. Eugene, 74, 156
Robins, A. W., 71
Robins Family, 14, 40, 42
Robins property, 40, 42,
Robins, Archibald, 42
Robins, Elizabeth, 110
Robins, John, 13, 40
Robins, Lucy, 111
Robins Mill, 42
Robins Neck, 40, 44, 46, 55, 63, 75, 77, 200
Robins, Robert, 148
Rochambeau, General, 38, 40
Rogers Company, 151
Rogers, William, 44
Rolfe, John, 16, 17
Rolfe, Thomas, 17
Rose, Dr., 47
Rosewell, 11, 34, 35, 36, 44, 58, 60, 130, 140, 149, 153, 170
Rosewell Foundation, 130, 170
Rowe, Kathryn, 110
Rowe, Lesbia, 110
Rudd, Bohmer, 111
Rudducks, 144
Ruitans Club, 129

S

Saddlers Neck, 46, 75
saltwater pool, 178
Sander's Commons, 128, 133
Sanders, Francis F., 133
Sanders, Van Bibber, 145
Sarahs Creek, 40, 106
school bus, 69, 98
Scott, Emmett, 155
Seafood Festivals, 129
Seawell, John B., 44
Seawell, John Tyler, 57
Seawell's Ordinary, 39, 173
Secession, 47, 57,
Second Virginia Convention, 34
Selden Family, 46, 144
Selden, Robert Colgate, 46
Seven Pines, 59
Seventh Regiment, 35
Severn Lodge, 173
Severn Presbyterian Church, 55
Severn River, 12, 15, 19, 29, 46, 75, 80, 159

206

Severnby, 46
Shabby Hall, 46
Shackelford, Alexander, 71, 79
Shelly, 11, 61, 96, 130, 152, 153, 194
Shelly Ford, 64
Shepherdsville Baptist Church, 52
Sherwood, 46, 48, 58, 66, 87,89, 100, 166
Sherwood's garden, 167
Shocking corn, 102
Short Lane, 131
Signpino, 68,
Simcoe, Colonel, 36
Sinclair Family, 192
Sinclair, George W., 69
Sinclair, Georgiana, 86
Sinclair, Indie, 139
Sinclair, Mr. and Mrs. James, 93
Sinclair, Jeff B., 118, 138
Sinclair, Jefferson K., 69
Sinclair, Major Jefferson, 44
Sinclair, Captain John, 44, 46
Sinclair, John Mackie, 96, 119
Sinclair, T. Jeff Jr., 185
Sinclair, T. Jefferson Sr., 185
Sinclair, Roy, 86
Sinclair, Wythe, 192, 193
Singleton Methodist Church, 54
slavery, 44, 45, 46, 47, 61, 74, 76
Smith, A. W., 71
Smith, Captain John, 11, 13, 17, 124
Smith, Thomas, 71
"snow days", 128
Snyder, Danny, 136
Social Service Department, 98
Southampton, England, 147
Speaker of the House, 17, 163
Spencer, Dr. J. Blair, 114
Spencer, Mrs. Minnie, 110
St. Paul's Baptist Church, 52
Stafford, S. Phillip, 138, 194
Stafford, S. Phillip, Jr., 139
Stamp Act, 34
Stanley, Dr. Gray, 133
"starving time", 11
State Fair, 144
Sterling, Edith, 110
Sterling, Rudolf, 69
Sterling, Mr. and Mrs. Sam, 99
Sterling, Samuel, E., 55
Sterlings, 159
still, 122
Stonewall, C.S.S., 62
Stubblefield, Evelyn, 111
Stubbs Collection 76
Stubbs Family, 27, 76
Stubbs, J. L., 71
Stubbs, James N., 71
Stubbs, Linwood, 110
Stubbs, Mr. and Mrs. William Carter, 76
Summerville, 66
Sunday School, 46, 54
Surrender, 55
surrender, 37, 38, 40, 47, 57, 59, 60, 62, 151
surrender at Yorktown, 14, 130
surrenders at Yorktown and Gloucester Point, 130

T

Tabb, Cassie, 93
Tabb, John Fisher, 87
Tabb, Dr. John Prosser, 177
Tabb, Mr., 66
Tabb, Mrs. Mary Mason, 53
Tabb, Phillip, 36, 93,
Taliaferro, Brigadier General William Booth, 59, 60
Taliaferro, Colonel William B., 58, 71, 176
Taliaferro Family, 28, 175
Taliaferro, James, L., 71
Taliaferro, Phillip, 176
Talliaferro Store, 77
Taliaferro, Thomas, S., 71
Taliaferro, Warner, 176
Tarleton, Lieutenant Colonel Banastre, 14, 36, 37, 38, 151
"Tea Party", 34
telephone building
telephone company, 74
Tercentennnial, 140
Thirty-second Virginia Infantry, 58
Thomas C. Walker Elementary School, 74, 109
Thornton, Cornelia, 95
Throckmorton, Robert, 13
Thruston, William, R., 71
tidal wave, 128
Tidewater Fox Hunt, 118
Tidewater Fox Hunt Association, 118, 129
Tidewater Telephone Company, 73
Timberneck, 35
Timberneck Farm, 15
tithes, 12
Todd, Thomas, 28, 198
Toddsbury, 28, 53, 173, 198
Tomkies Family, 47, 178
Tomkies, Robert, 36
Tom's Bridge, 25
Tom's Hill School, 25
Tournaments, 45, 85, 119
Townshend Act, 34
Treaty of Ghent (1814), 45
Treaty of Paris, 37
Trevilian, A. T., 77
Triangle Squares, 150
Tricentennial, 150
trot lines, 105
True Blooded Yankee, USS, 57, 58
Tucker, Bishop Henry St. George, 128
Tyndall Park, 65
Tyndall's Point, 13

U

Union Baptist Chruch 46, 50

V

Valley Campaign, 59
Valley Front, 66, 76
Victory Center, 37
Violet Bank, 15
Virginia, 153
Virginia Boats (Navy), 34
Virginia Constitutional Convention, 57
Virginia Council, 33
Virginia Fisheries Laboratory, 129, 131
Virginia Institute of Marine Science, 129, 131, 153, 187
Virginia Landmark, 19, 29, 36, 153, 155, 173
Virginia Museum, 140
Virginia Navy, 35
Virginia Register of Historic Places, 28
Virginia State Library, 131
Volunteer Fire Departments, 163

W

Waddell, Burford, 111
Waddell, William, 71
Waldrop, M. A., 110
Walker, George Washington, 71
Walker, Grace, 109
Walker, Thomas Calhoun, 45, 74, 109, 176
Washington, George Walker, 71
Wallace, Severn, 138
Walter Reed Memorial Hospital, 128
Walton, B. L. Sr., 114
Walton, Dennis, 114
Waonda Farm, 114
War Between the States, 64
War of 1812, 45
War of Independence, 37
Ware Academy, 195
Ware Chuch, 18, 38, 45, 50, 58, 61, 64, 140, 173
Ware Neck, 54, 75, 77
Ware parish, 12, 29
Ware River, 12, 28, 84, 114, 178
Ware River Yacht Club, 187
Warehouse, 30
Warehouse Landing, 30, 184
Warner, Augustine, 13, 19
Warner Hall, 14, 19, 38, 44, 46, 60
Warner-Lewis Family, 19
Warsaw, 141
Washington, Booker T., 155
Washington Family, 14
Washington, General George, 14, 36, 37, 38, 39
Washington, John, 38

Waterman's Hall, 153
Watermen's Museum, 154
Weedon, General, 37
weirs, 104
Wellness and Fitness Center, 128
West Point, 103
Whaley, Michael, 151
White Hall, 140, 144
White Marsh, 60, 61, 93, 128
White Marsh Plantation, 181
Whiting Family, 14
Whiting, Thomas, 34, 35, 36, 43
Whitley, William, 151
Whittakers Creek, 159
Wiatt, Alexander, 12, 138, 194
Wiatt, A. T., 71
Wiatt, The Reverend William E., 50, 51,61
Wiatt Family, 68
Wiatt, Laura Campbell, 62
Wiatt, William E., 71
Wicomico, 108
Williams, John, 71
Williams, William T., 71
Williamsburg, 14, 34, 35
Willis Family, 47
Willis, Francis, 47, 140
Wilson's Creek, 188
Windsor, 41
Woman's Club Building, 22
women at home, 64
Woods Cross Roads, 68
Works Progress Admininstration, 98, 173
World War I, 76, 95, 96, 97
World War II, 98, 99, 116, 127, 129, 130

Y

York, 75, 123, 127
York Monument, 22, 47
Yorktown, 58, 59

Z

Zion Poplars Baptist Church, 51

207

Caroline Baytop Sinclair, educator and author, is a native of Gloucester County and had a home there until she retired to Westminster-Canterbury in Richmond in 1982. She earned a B. S. at the College of William and Mary, Phi Beta Kappa, and a Ph.D. at New York University.

Dr. Sinclair retired from James Madison University (formerly Madison College) where she was Professor and Head of the Department of Health and Physical Education. Having taught in the public schools and other colleges of Virginia and other states, she won recognition in her chosen profession and was elected to state, regional and national office and honors. After leaving James Madison University, Dr. Sinclair lived at her home in Gloucester. She did a four-year research project in Richmond and became deeply involved in the Historical and Bicentennial programs of Gloucester County.

As a writer Dr. Sinclair always contributed to professional literature. Since her retirement she has written six books. They are: *Movement of the Young Child, Ages Two to Six*; *The Kidknapped Child*, a fictional biography, and four based on Gloucester's history, *Stories of Old Gloucester*; *Abingdon Church, A Chronology of its History, 1650–1970*; *The Four Families of Rosewell*; and *Gloucester's Past in Pictures*.

Explanation

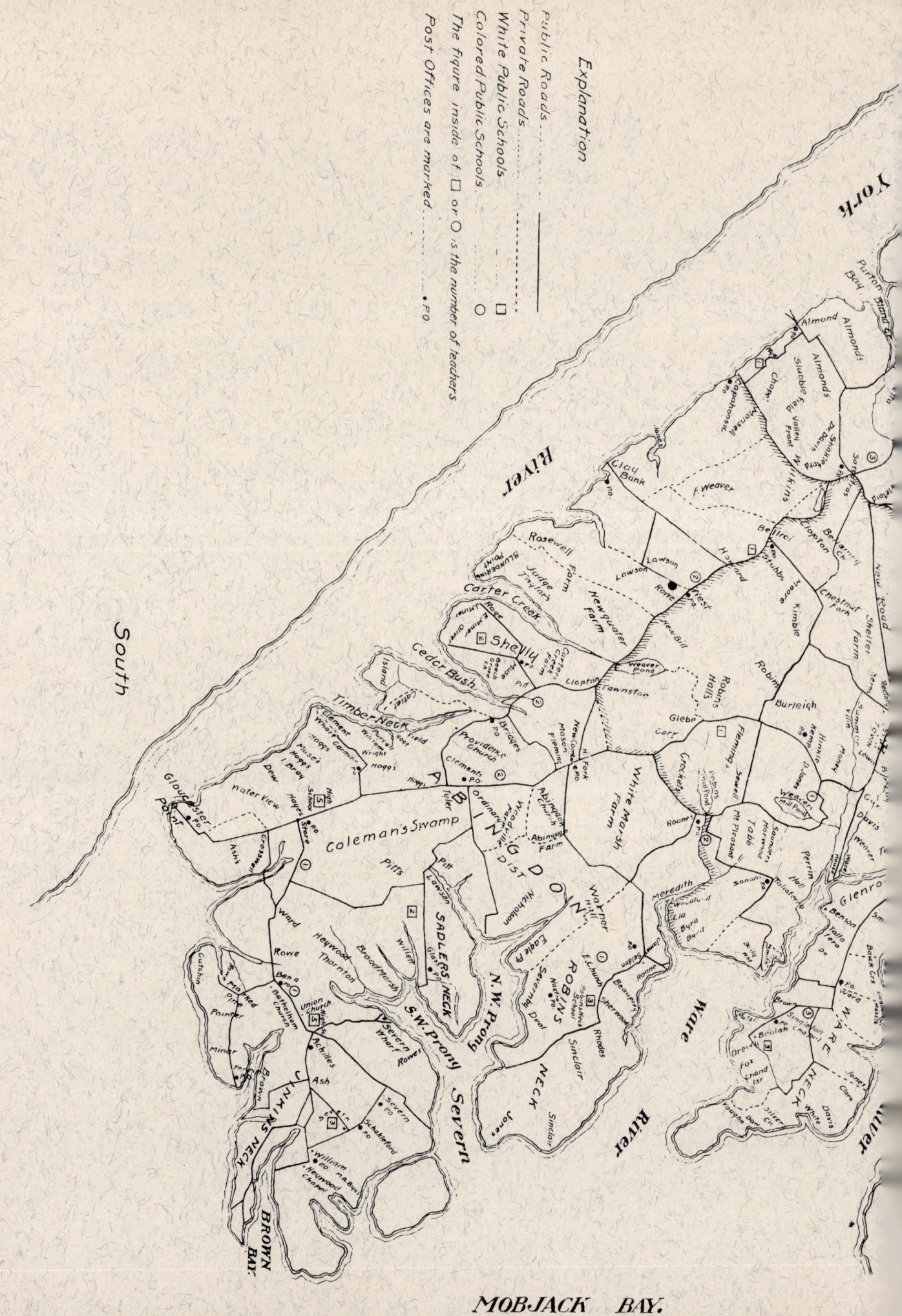

Public Roads ....
Private Roads ....
White Public Schools .... ☐
Colored Public Schools .... ○
The figure inside of ☐ or ○ is the number of teachers
Post Offices are marked .... P.O.

MOBJACK BAY.